Consider It Sold

Home Staging Strategies
for a
Quick and Profitable Sale

By
Shannon Weber and **Joanne Sanche**

This book is dedicated to the memory of
Shannon's late colleague and dear friend,
Dr. Patty Witzel.

Consider It Sold

Home Staging Strategies for a Quick and Profitable Sale
By Shannon Weber and Joanne Sanche

Published by IFO Press
E-mail: infineorder@sasktel.net

Original photography by Danny Classen.
Cover photo by Hans Holtkamp.

ISBN, print ed. 978-0-9879302-0-0
ISBN, PDF ed. 978-0-9879302-1-7
ISBN, eBook ed. 978-0-9879302-2-4

Contents

Part One
Building the Foundation

Part Two
The Four-Step Home Staging Plan

Part Three
Almost Showtime!

Preface

If you're thinking about selling your house, then you've most likely heard about home staging. Until relatively recently, staging has been a well-kept secret of savvy sellers and real estate agents. With the advent of home decorating and real estate programs on TV, however, more homeowners are becoming aware of the benefits of staging their home before putting it on the market.

Staging is a truly effective way to persuade potential buyers that your house is the one for them. Regardless of where you live, how big or small your home is, its listing price, or the number of people living in it, the same basic staging principles apply. Staging will improve the perceived value of your home and will help it sell quickly and profitably.

You might wonder how can we give advice on making changes to your home when we haven't even seen it. The fact is, we all fill our homes with beloved treasures and choose paint, art, furniture, and accessories to express our personal style. After all, a house is a private space, arranged to suit the homeowner's needs and tastes. However, the way you normally live in your home is not usually the best way to sell it. Staging is not about making your house nicer, more convenient, or more comfortable for yourself. It's about showcasing it so potential buyers can clearly see the space, appreciate its best features, and want to snap it up.

This book demystifies the staging process and will guide you through it from beginning to end. It is divided into three parts:

- Part 1, "Building the Foundation," is an introduction to home staging. It clearly describes what it is (hint: it involves psychology and is more about marketing than decorating), its benefits, and when you should begin the process. You'll discover how to prepare for the staging process, including examining your feelings about moving, assessing your home and the competition, and setting a timeline and budget. You'll also get tips on motivating yourself to get the job done.

- Part 2, "The Four-Step Home Staging Plan," thoroughly details how to stage your house in four steps: de-cluttering and depersonalizing, making simple repairs and upgrades, cleaning, and styling. It explains the principles behind the process so you can apply them to suit your unique needs. It shares our favorite online shopping sites for first-rate staging supplies, and each chapter includes a detailed checklist to help you keep organized.

- Part 3, "Almost Showtime," addresses how to stage the exterior of your house for excellent curb appeal. You'll also get tips for special situations, such as staging a vacant house, seasonal staging considerations, and how to stage your house quickly when you're in a rush to put it on the market. Finally, you'll learn the basics of photographing your house for online postings and stress-relieving strategies for maintaining and showing your staged house. You'll find more checklists to guide through these finishing touches.

Going through the home staging process is not always easy. There will be moments when you doubt whether some of the suggested changes could possibly make a difference (they will). You might even find it hard to implement changes and see your house in a new way. We feel your pain. However, some parts of the staging process are actually fun, and many people like the results so much that they continue using many of the staging principles in their new homes.

We can assure you that home staging does work: compared to non-staged competitors, staged homes are more attractive to more buyers and therefore sell quicker and for more money. Your home was a major purchase, and your money was hard earned. Staging it to sell offers a solid opportunity to profit from your investment.

PART ONE

Building the Foundation

So, you're moving. Feeling stressed? It's no wonder if you are. The issues associated with moving can be physically and emotionally draining. Many people find that moving creates an enormous amount of work, stress, and upheaval in their lives. This is where home staging can help. Smart staging techniques will not only attract interested buyers and hasten a sale in any market, they will also help keep you organized and prepared for moving day. The following two chapters are a general introduction to home staging and an explanation of what you need to do before you begin staging your house.

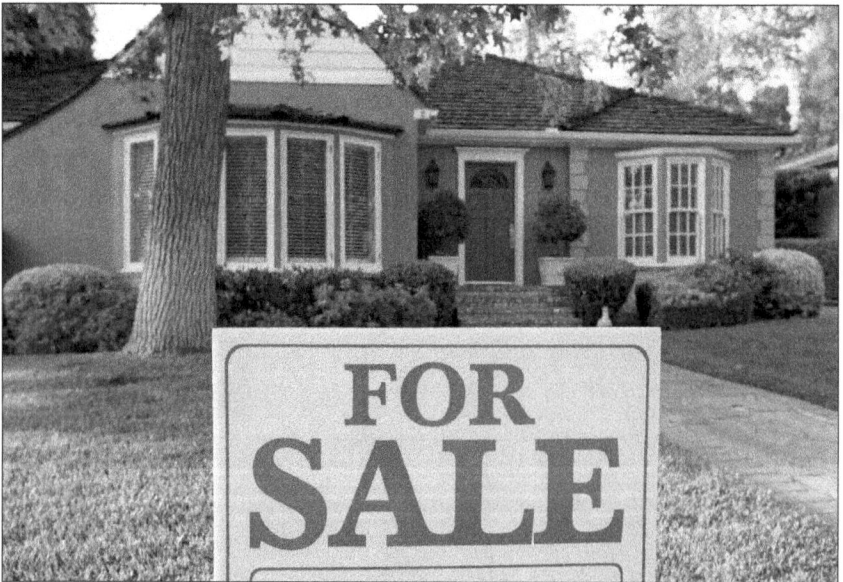

chapter one

An Introduction to Home Staging

FOR MOST HOMEOWNERS, their house is their most valuable asset. When the time comes to move, they want to sell it for top price. All too often, however, they rush to put their house on the market and are surprised and disappointed when it doesn't sell right away. If the house sits on the market for too long, the seller either has to take it off for a while or reduce the list price, oftentimes drastically, and sacrifice thousands or tens of thousands of dollars.

Many factors affect housing sales, many of which are out of the homeowner's control, such as total number of houses on the market, mortgage rates, unemployment rates, and regional housing values. However, two crucial factors that significantly affect time on market are completely within the homeowner's control: the **asking price** and the **presentation of the house**. Your real estate agent will help you determine a reasonable asking price. This book will help you with the presentation of your house.

What Is Home Staging?

"Time and again, we find that staging our new homes significantly decreases the number of days they're on the market."

Kelly Oleksyn, Mosaic Developments Corp.

Home staging involves making simple yet strategic changes to a house before it's listed so that it appeals to the greatest number of buyers. The more buyers attracted to a house, the better the chance of a quick sale. And a quick sale usually means a more profitable sale. This is because buyers know that when a house sits on the market for a few weeks, the seller is more open to negotiation than when the house is first listed. Thus, the longer a house sits on the market, the lower the offer price relative to the list price.

You need to persuade potential buyers that your house offers exceptional value. Buyers often underestimate the value of a house simply because of problems with the way it is presented. By carefully staging your home, you will improve upon many details, some seemingly minor, which together will greatly increase its perceived value. Your staging efforts will make buyers notice your home and love what they see.

Home staging goes well beyond the obvious chores of tidying the house and mowing the lawn before a showing. As you'll learn in this book, it includes a wide variety of tasks, from making needed repairs to creating focal points in a room. None of these tasks are complicated, but many require time and effort.

Your staging work will give you a distinct edge in the real estate market. A staged home has excellent curb appeal outside and looks spacious, clean, orderly, and up-to-date inside. Most of all, it is so appealing that potential buyers will want to linger and dream about living there. And once you have people imagining living in your house, it won't be long before you get an offer.

How Home Staging Appeals to Buyer Psychology

Buying a house is a surprisingly emotional decision. Even though it's a significant investment, we usually make relatively quick decisions based on first impressions, gut feelings, and intuition. Buyers often decide whether or not they like a house within the first few minutes, sometimes even the first few seconds, of walking in the door. After the deal is complete, people often explain their decision using emotional terms: they just "felt" the house was right for them, or they immediately "fell in love" with it.

It's All in the Details

Don't believe that small, subtle details can influence people's decisions?

In his book *59 Seconds: Think a Little, Change a Lot,* psychologist and author Richard Wiseman lists numerous studies showing that seemingly insignificant details can influence people's behaviours. For example, researchers found that after people sat in front of a computer screen that had dollar signs as its wallpaper, they subsequently were less likely to donate to charity and were less friendly to others; interviewers who were given cold cups of coffee tended to rate their interviewees as "colder and less pleasant"; and people who saw a briefcase on a table during a meeting suddenly became more competitive.

Buyers make snap decisions because they tend to make broad assumptions, often subconsciously, based on subtle visual cues. What buyers see, and subsequently feel, when viewing a house strongly influences whether they make an offer. For instance, if buyers see a cluttered or overflowing closet, they assume that the house doesn't have enough storage space. Similarly, if they see minor issues like a cracked window, peeling paint, or a messy room, they assume that the house has not been well maintained and that other, more significant problems may arise. Of course, people don't usually realize they are making such assumptions, but they leave with a feeling of unease and may not even know why.

On the other hand, other visual details can create feelings of well-being and comfort, like a cozy reading corner, fresh flowers, or a spacious room with plenty of natural sunlight. Home stagers understand that small details make big impressions and carefully stage the house to make a stunning first impression, draw buyers in, and make them want to stay.

Home staging exploits what Dan Ariely, author and professor of psychology and behavioral economics at MIT, describes as the principle of "virtual ownership." People tend to value something more when they own it. Even if we simply imagine owning something, we place greater value on it. The advertising industry has discovered this concept a long time ago. We see a commercial showing a happy family going to a soccer game in a minivan, and we imagine ourselves in their place. We already start thinking of it as ours as we plan where everyone would sit and how we would use the extra cargo space under the seat.

A properly staged house is presented so that buyers will be inclined to imagine themselves and their families living there. And when they imagine living there, they already assume virtual ownership and thus become more emotionally attached to the house and more likely to buy it.

Staging also appeals to people's natural desire to improve the quality of their lives. People looking for a new house are usually looking to "move up." Even if they're downsizing, most people hope to move to a place that is in some way better than where they currently are living. For most people, "better" means more space, more storage, and less work. Staging your house will convince potential buyers that it is a spacious, serene place where everything they need is already waiting for them.

Of course, people know that every house requires upkeep and cleaning. They understand that children with sticky fingers or dogs with muddy paws invariably leave their marks on the walls and floors. However, your house doesn't need to remind them of these realities. No, your house will seem as if it's so well organized, clutter is not an issue; it's so well maintained that repairs will never be a problem; and it's so clean that surely it must practically clean itself. In other words, you're selling a dream.

What Home Staging Is Not

Because home staging is still a relatively new field, there are some misconceptions about it. The following are examples of what home staging is *not*:

- **Home staging is not the same as home decorating.** While it's true that home staging creates a lovely looking house, the goals of home staging are very different than the goals of home decorating. Decorating involves styling your house to reflect your tastes and personality and to suit your needs. Home staging involves removing signs of your presence or unique taste in order to create a neutral space. The goal is to show off the best features of the house, not to express your creativity or personality. Forget about making your house comfortable or convenient for yourself. In fact, a staged house can be uncomfortable or inconvenient to live in because it is designed to meet the wants and needs of potential buyers, not the wants and needs of the owners.

- **Home staging is not deceptive.** The purpose of staging a house is to highlight its best features while minimizing its flaws. Staging isn't about hiding problems or deceiving people. It is unethical (and possibly illegal) to hide a problem or defect rather than repair it or disclose it to the buyer. Simply put, staging serves to present a house so that it is visually and emotionally appealing to the greatest number of potential buyers.

The Benefits of Home Staging

"I recently had a house on an excellent crescent that just wasn't generating interest from buyers. After a few months I convinced the owners to have it staged. What a remarkable difference! The comments from potential buyers immediately changed from being negative to very complimentary, and it sold very soon afterward."

Ron Baliski, Ron Baliski Realty Inc., Re/Max

People stage their homes for two main reasons: profit and convenience.

According to studies released in 2010 by the Real Estate Staging Association (RESA), staged homes spend significantly less time on the market than non-staged homes. In their study, RESA followed 126 non-staged, unsold houses that had been on the market for an average of nine months (approximately 263 days). When the homeowners took these houses off the market, staged them, and then re-listed, these same houses then sold within about two months (60 days). In another study that same year, RESA found that houses that were staged before being placed on the market sold within about 39 days. This means that in RESA's study, houses staged prior to listing sold over six times faster than non-staged houses.

Consider the implications of selling your house quickly. Not only will you get more money (the US Department of Housing and Urban Development found that staged houses sell for up to 17% more than non-staged houses), you also will likely avoid having to move before your house is sold. The first few months in a new house are expensive, and carrying two mortgages would force many families into debt.

Selling your house quickly may also allow you to finalize the purchase of your new house. Putting the money from your previous house towards the new mortgage will also save you substantial interest costs.

While everyone wants to sell their house for the best price possible, most sellers also want the convenience of a quick sale so they can get on with their lives. Imagine being able to move when you want to and not having to put your life on hold until your house sells. Imagine the convenience of having fewer showings and fewer mad rushes to clean the house and put everything in order at a moment's notice.

Finally, home staging also helps to make moving day less stressful. As you'll see later in this chapter, part of home staging involves cleaning, de-cluttering, and packing away items that you don't immediately need. Doing these tasks well before moving day helps to spread out the enormous amount of work required to relocate. You will certainly appreciate the convenience of having a good portion of your packing and cleaning done early.

When is Home Staging Necessary?

"We strongly recommend home staging to the majority of our clients. In our experience, not only does the home show better, it subsequently sells quicker and for more money than properties that haven't been staged."

Barb Wouters, Mark Wouters Realty Inc., Re/Max

Virtually every homeowner wanting to improve the chances of a quick and profitable sale can benefit from home staging. We believe that home staging is always necessary:

- **Regardless of the market.** In a slow market, competition for buyers is very high. Staging your house will help it outshine the competition. In a hot real estate market, houses sell faster and easier. The better your home looks, the greater the chance you will receive multiple offers and a higher selling price.

- **Regardless of the neighbourhood.** Staging is becoming standard in some larger cities, especially in neighbourhoods with more costly homes. If the houses in your market are staged, then your competition is stiffer and you'll also need to stage your house in order to keep up. In other areas, homeowners may know nothing of staging and simply present their homes for sale as they have decorated and lived in them. If staging is not yet a popular selling strategy in your area, then enjoy the advantage you will clearly have by staging your home.

- **Whatever the style, price, and condition of the home.** Whether you live in a small condominium, a modest bungalow, or a large luxury home, staging is essential before listing. Smaller houses look more spacious after being staged. Homes in the higher price ranges have a smaller pool of potential buyers, so they must make very positive first impressions to meet buyers' high expectations. Every home has personal or disorganized areas that are not ready for showing. Even the cleanest and most up-to-date house can usually still benefit from some tweaking before being put on the market.

- **Whether the home is occupied or vacant.** Vacant homes are more challenging to sell because they tend to look cold and unwelcoming. Staging a vacant home by renting or borrowing furniture and accessories for key rooms will help it sell much quicker.

When to Stage Your Home

Start thinking about staging your home as soon as you make the decision to sell. Beginning right away leaves time to properly prepare and allows you to spread the work out over days, weeks, and even months.

Ideally, stage your home before:

- **Showing it to a real estate agent and setting a listing price.** Like anyone else, real estate agents are influenced by a staged home. The agent will be judging the house to determine a listing price, so prepare as much as you can before the first visit. Also, real estate agents tend to show staged homes more often because they know these homes are very appealing to buyers.

- **Posting photos of it on the MLS or other Internet listings.** It is essential to stage your home before posting any pictures of it online. According to the National Association of Realtors, 94% of buyers aged 24 to 44 uses the Internet to search for a house. The vast majority of buyers begin their search process online, even before contacting a real estate agent. Your photos will be the first contact you make with potential buyers. If they don't like what they see in the photos, they will simply move on to the next posting and not bother viewing your house in person. If you have already posted pictures before you have finished staging, it's not too late to replace these photos with new, post-staging photos. (Chapter 9 discusses how to photograph your staged house).

- **Open houses and private showings.** Ensure your house is staged before each potential buyer views it. This means refreshing your staging efforts before every single showing so that it looks just as good as it does in the photographs. (Chapter 9 provides tips on maintaining your staged house so that last-minute showings will be a snap.)

Of course, you can also stage your home when you are not selling it. Once people see the simple, low-cost, yet dramatic improvements that staging makes, they often want to stage their new homes to create the ideal space for themselves. You can easily adapt many of the home staging steps and principles to make your new (or lived-in) home more organized, updated, and stylish.

chapter two

Preparations Before Staging

NOW IS THE TIME TO MAKE A STAGING PLAN. This chapter outlines preparations to consider before you start staging. You might be surprised to learn that the first task is to examine your thoughts and feelings about your upcoming move.

Emotionally Detach From Your Home

Frequently, one of the biggest obstacles to staging is the homeowner's reluctance to make changes. Why would anyone wanting to sell her home resist making changes that would make it easier to sell? Often, even though she may not realize this, it's because she is emotionally attached to her home and is reluctant to move.

Moving can stir up complex emotions; rarely is it easy to leave your home or neighbourhood. After all, moving is a major life change. Even if you're looking forward to a new future, you're still leaving a phase of your life behind, which is never easy. Everyone mourns loss, and moving involves dealing with a significant amount of loss.

If home was a refuge and comfort, saying good-bye can bring up feelings of sadness and grief. Most people feel nostalgia for the good times and all the "firsts" that happened there. If home was associated with conflict and strife, there may be feelings of relief in leaving but also disappointment and regret in leaving a place that didn't live up to hopes and expectations. People often must move because of distressing events such as divorce, death of a spouse, or financial difficulties. In these cases, moving away from a loved home and community is even more difficult and may feel like yet another loss.

Once you make the decision to sell your home (or, if the decision was thrust upon you, once you accept that you must sell), it is critical to begin a process of letting go of your deep attachments to the house. Sellers who are still emotionally attached to their homes have a very difficult time being objective about it, and objectivity is critical for making the right staging choices.

If you are not objective about the condition of your home, your biases towards it will cloud your judgment. Remember, ownership causes us to attach greater value to an object, often leading us to overlook its imperfections. For example, the faux paint finishes and stenciling that you painstakingly added in the '90s may bring warm memories and still look fine to you. Maybe you have lived with a broken closet door for years and are so used to kicking it closed that you no longer even notice it. Perhaps you're so used to the brass and smoked glass lighting fixtures that came with the house that you forget they're there. Potential buyers, however, don't have any attachments to your house and will quickly notice flaws and outdated features.

Allow yourself to feel your feelings while gradually beginning to view your home more objectively. Even a slight shift in thinking can have a profound effect. For example, instead of thinking "this is my home," think, "this is a house." Try changing your perspective from "I live here" to "I will be leaving." Move from "this is mine" to "I want someone else to have this." For some, this will happen naturally and quickly. For others, letting go may take longer and require patience and effort.

Acknowledge your feelings about moving, whether you are feeling excitement, relief, disappointment, sadness, or a combination of all of them. Remind yourself that these feelings are natural. It can be helpful to confide in someone you trust and plan ways to move forward appropriately.

Strategies to Help You Move On

The following are some methods you might want to try to help you through the process of letting go:

- Take pictures of your home before it is staged so you can remember it just as it was. After it is staged, it may no longer seem like your house. Remember to take pictures of your yard too.

- Throw a family "good-bye party" for your house. Include the children, and invite everyone to talk about their favorite memories of the house.

- Record a "walking tour" of your house and yard. You or your family could narrate this as you go along, recording special memories or comments about each room.

- Write a note to leave for the new owners, detailing what you know about the house's history and maybe a little bit about your life there. You could include some pictures of the house through the years to show how it has changed. Wish them well in their new home.

- Hide a time capsule or leave a small memento in the house. For example, if you have a hole in the wall that needs repair, hide a photo or note inside it before patching. People who have left messages say they found it comforting to think someone might find these little treasures years from now.

- Spend some time imagining your new home. Get excited about everything that you can look forward to. Are you eagerly anticipating moving to a larger home or more convenient location? Focus on how moving will be the beginning of a new chapter of your life.

Eventually, you need to consider your property as a valuable asset, a product that you need to package and market. While this sounds cold, it can actually help you move forward with your staging work. Making your house look its best is a way to honor the time you spent there and to show buyers that this house has been loved and nurtured.

Check Out the Competition

Another important task to do before staging is to check out your competition—the other houses for sale in your area that are comparable in size and price to your house. These homeowners are trying to capture the same buyer that you are. Knowing what these houses are like will tell you what features buyers will be expecting for the price. Try to meet and, if possible, exceed buyers' expectations. Keep in mind, however, that you shouldn't over-improve your property. For example, if none of your competitors have hardwood flooring or granite countertops, adding these features to your house will not likely pay off.

There are many ways to see what other sellers are offering. The best place to begin is on the Internet. Find houses in your general area that are comparable to yours. You can read about the features of these homes and check posted photographs and virtual tours. It's also a good idea to drop in on some open houses. Notice what features these houses offer. Is your home up to their standards? Ask yourself how you can present a better product and win over buyers.

Consider the kind of impression the competitor house makes. When looking at it, think about the following:

- What is the yard like? Is the exterior of the house in good shape?
- Is the home cluttered and messy or is it well organized, spacious, and free of personal items?
- Does the home look modern or dated? Does it need any work, or is it move-in ready?
- How many bedrooms and bathrooms are included? What are their size and condition?
- What is the condition of the kitchen? Does it have special features like granite countertops, an island, or a large pantry?
- Has the house been recently updated (e.g., fresh paint, new fixtures, hardwood flooring)?
- Is the basement finished?
- Is the garage large and tidy?
- Is there enough storage space?
- How clean is the house? Does it smell clean and fresh?

Assess Your House

Now that you know what your competition offers, ensure that your house offers just as much or more. Think about where your place needs improvement and focus your staging efforts there. If your house is better than the competition, think about how you can highlight these advantages. In other words, stage your house to improve or detract from its weaknesses and to show off its advantages.

> ## A Word of Caution about Home Improvements
>
> The goal of this book is to guide you through the home staging process, which involves minor repairs, simple upgrades, and generally using what you already have to its best advantage. Home staging does not involve undertaking major home renovations, such as remodeling a kitchen or building an addition.
>
> Sometimes major renovations add significant value to the price of a house; oftentimes, however, they don't add enough value to recoup the money invested. Many variables affect whether a renovation improves resale value. Research carefully before deciding whether a major renovation will help you sell your home. Discuss with a real estate professional whether adjusting your asking price would be more profitable than sinking money into a renovation.
>
> We will help you focus on changes, other than major renovations, that will help your house sell for top dollar. There are many simple, quick, and inexpensive (many free) ways to greatly improve the presentation of your home.

Ideally, read through this book before assessing your home. Once you have a good understanding of what's involved in home staging, you can better decide what's needed for your house. When assessing your house, it's crucial to be completely objective. If possible, ask a friend to help you with this task.

Begin by standing in each doorway in your home and evaluating your impression of the space before you. Imagine that you are seeing it for the first time. Ask yourself, "What will people see here?" Keep in mind your impressions when you checked out the competition. Compared to those houses, does yours seem spacious or cluttered? Is it organized and serene or messy and chaotic? Is it bright and welcoming or dark and dreary? Is its style neat and up-to-date or old-fashioned and dingy? Do any problems catch your attention, such as dents in the walls or cracked windows? Write a list of everything that needs work.

You could also take pictures from various places in the room and then assess what you see in the photos. Pictures don't lie, and you may be able to see a room with greater objectivity in a photo than you would otherwise.

Finally, assess the smell of your home. Every house has a unique smell that the homeowner often doesn't even notice. Numerous factors cause odors, including foods, pets, cigarette smoke, dust, and mold or mildew. If a house looks great but has a noticeable odor, it will be very difficult to sell. The smell in the house will be the first greeting as buyers step in. Make sure that your house has a pleasant and fresh smell. A good way to assess for odors is to ask someone who doesn't live in the house to give you a brutally honest opinion.

Set a Timeline

Once you have your list of what needs to be done, decide when you want your house to be ready and how much you can complete before this deadline.

The best-case scenario is that you have weeks to months to prepare your home, you have energetic and enthusiastic family and friends to help, and you complete the work before the "For Sale" sign is on your lawn. In reality, you likely have a busy life, friends and family members who are also busy, and limited time before listing your home. Don't despair. This book is designed to simplify the staging process, keep you organized and motivated, and reveal many handy tips to save time and energy.

First, be honest about the state of your home. If you have a small, well-maintained home and a weekly housekeeper, you'll likely need less time to stage it. Maybe you only need a few weekends to finish everything.

If you have a busy family life and many other commitments, chances are you have fewer blocks of time to devote to staging and will require 4 to 6 weeks to get the work done. If you need to hire professionals, for example, to replace worn carpets or install new countertops, expect to set aside at least two months, depending on how quickly you can get service. Because it will likely take more time than anticipated, shoot for an over-estimation.

Next, be honest about how much you can do on your own. Determine what you can reasonably do yourself and where others might help. Can friends and family help? Do you need to hire a professional staging team? Is it more reasonable to partially stage at first and then continue after listing? Whatever the answers to these questions, remember that many aspects of staging (i.e., de-cluttering, packing, and cleaning) will save time and effort later on and make moving out much easier.

Set Your Priorities

It's easy to get overwhelmed when you see a long to-do list. Don't panic. It isn't realistic or even necessary to do everything suggested in this book. Although staging has a tremendous impact, you don't have to stage the entire house to make a difference. Even small and simple changes in key areas can influence buyers and help sell the house. Chapter 8 gives useful shortcuts for when time is limited.

Prioritize your to-do list by focusing on the most obvious issues and the problems that are the easiest to fix. Because first impressions are critical, pay particular attention to staging the areas that buyers see first, generally in the following order:

- Front exterior of your house and front yard (see Chapter 7)
- Front entryway and areas that you can see when you step inside the front door
- Kitchen/dining room
- Main living areas (living room, family room, or great room)
- Bathrooms
- Bedrooms (master bedroom first, and then the others)
- Closets and storage spaces

- Den/office
- Laundry area
- Basement
- Backyard
- Garage

When you're ready to start staging, follow the steps in the order that they are discussed in this book, focusing on one task at a time.

Try to finish the first three staging steps (de-cluttering, repairing/upgrading, and cleaning) well ahead of listing your home; as soon as you decide to move, get started on them. Complete the fourth step (styling) shortly before you meet your real estate agent, set a list price, take photographs, and show your home.

Of course, upkeep is essential until the house is sold. Keep your house looking freshly staged for each and every showing. Chapter 9 describes how to maintain a staged house.

Set a Budget

"I greatly appreciate how budget-friendly home staging was for us. We purchased very little, mainly using furniture and accents that we already owned and just arranging them in new ways. It IS possible to make your home look beautiful and professionally designed without spending a lot of money!"

Melanie Orvold, homeowner

Many people are reluctant to spend money before selling, hoping to save as much as possible to invest in their new home. Others wonder why they should put any more money into a house that they're going to sell; after all, the new owners can update the house however they want. This thinking limits the possibilities for presenting an impressive property that will bring a solid return. Spending a bit in key areas (the exterior, kitchen, bathrooms, and main living area) can often prompt a quick and profitable sale.

How much you spend depends on the condition of your home. Typically, people who do their own home staging invest up to 1% of their asking price. Most of this money goes towards hiring professionals and completing repairs and upgrades.

Staging doesn't have to cost a lot of money, though. We will show you some smart, inexpensive strategies you can use to stage your house. Unless a house has been severely neglected, extreme spending is not necessary. Outside of significant repairs and updates, most staging work requires only your time, some elbow grease, and a little creativity. This "free" work makes an enormous difference in the appearance of your home and can hasten its sale.

Stay Motivated

Knowing what needs to be done and getting it done are two entirely different matters.

Let's face it, many staging tasks require a lot of work and determination. Some may seem like pure drudgery. Especially if you have a lot to do, you could easily become overwhelmed and give up. It's important to motivate yourself to complete as much as possible.

Psychologist and author Richard Wiseman identified the following five simple techniques that can help anyone keep on task. Try using them to keep yourself motivated when staging your house:

- **Make a plan consisting of small steps that you can complete within a specific time frame.** Plan everything you want to accomplish to stage your house within a realistic time frame. Record your plan. If necessary, break each job down into small, easily accomplished tasks and create interim deadlines along the way. For example, instead of trying to de-clutter the entire basement, focus on one very small area at a time, such as the storage room in the basement. If necessary, make the tasks ridiculously small and easy to accomplish, such as tidying one shelf in the storage room in the basement. Accomplishing a task, no matter how small, will motivate you to continue.

- **Tell other people about your plan.** Post on your Facebook page, tweet, text, or simply tell family, friends, and colleagues about reading this book and what you're planning to do to stage your house. Wiseman explains that going public with their plans makes people more invested in achieving them. It also may result in family and friends offering encouragement and support.

- **Remind yourself of the good things that will happen if you complete your plan.** Remind yourself often of the benefits of staging your house. As you're scouring grout, tell yourself that you're doing this to sell your house quicker and for more money. Imagine that every item that you pack away represents money in the bank. If necessary, change your mindset. Instead of thinking "I have to," tell yourself "I want to" or "I can."

- **Reward yourself when you complete each step.** Have something to look forward to by rewarding yourself after completing each task. This may be as simple as going to a movie, having a gourmet coffee, or taking a walk. Keep your rewards healthy, and don't overdo rewarding yourself with food. Don't reward yourself with unnecessary purchases, either, or you could end up creating more clutter. Also reward yourself as you're doing the task by making it fun. For instance, listen to some music while you're cleaning or ask a friend to help and you might enjoy the companionship as much as the help.

- **Record your progress (e.g., in a journal or on a chart).** Keep a daily written record of your progress. You might be pleasantly surprised by how much you accomplish. If you print out and use the checklists included in this book, add a checkmark as you complete each task. Seeing the checkmarks add up will inspire you to continue.

Stop Procrastinating Now

In his book *59 Seconds: Think a Little, Change a Lot*, Richard Wiseman describes the Zeigarnik Effect, the theory that people tend to remember interrupted and unfinished tasks better than completed ones. He explains that starting an activity causes many people to experience a type of "psychic anxiety" that isn't relieved until the activity is complete. In other words, once you start an activity, your mind usually nags you until you finish it.

How does this relate to home staging? People who are overwhelmed by the amount of tasks on their to-do list tend to procrastinate and may never begin. Research shows that when procrastinators force themselves to work on a task "just a few minutes," however, they often feel compelled to see it through to completion. Those few minutes starting the project create an "anxious brain" that isn't relieved until the job is done.

So, if you tend to procrastinate so much that you don't even start a staging project, try the "just a few minutes" rule. Tell yourself you'll wash the kitchen walls for five minutes, and then don't be surprised if you end up doing the kitchen, hallway, and living room walls as well! Master the art of starting, and before you know it, you'll be finishing.

PART TWO

The Four-Step Home Staging Plan

This section details our four-step home staging plan, with each chapter focusing on one of the steps: de-cluttering and depersonalizing (check out the De-cluttering Decision Tree in the Appendix); repairing and upgrading; cleaning; and styling with furniture, art, and accessories. You might need to focus more on some steps than others; however, even small changes can make a big difference. Complete at least some of each of the steps described in the next four chapters, and you'll be assured of a superb presentation when you list your home. And a superb presentation increases the likelihood of a quicker sale at a higher price.

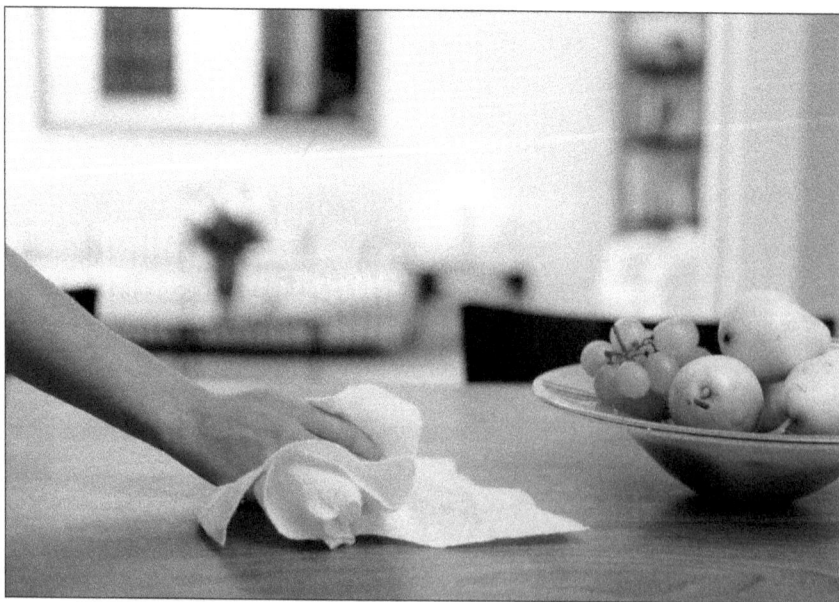

chapter three

Step 1: De-Cluttering and Depersonalizing

TO FAIRLY JUDGE A HOUSE and to fully appreciate it, buyers need to clearly see its layout and key features, also called its "bones." However, sellers often create distractions that prevent buyers from truly seeing the house. The most common distractions are clutter and personalized belongings.

The late comedian George Carlin had it right when he said, "Have you ever noticed when you visit some else's house, you never quite feel at home? You know why? No room for your stuff! Somebody *else's* stuff is all over the place." Buyers need to be able to focus on the room, not on the "stuff" in the room, no matter how lovely the stuff may be.

Most of us have acquired too much stuff. It's easy to amass collections, mementoes, books, knick-knacks, clothes, photos, and even furniture. By minimizing clutter and personalized items, you'll free up much-needed space and encourage buyers to leave thinking about the house, not about you or the things in your house.

The first step to staging your home, therefore, is to de-clutter and depersonalize it.

You might worry that depersonalizing and de-cluttering will make your house too plain and boring. However, remember that your house is no longer your home but is a product to sell. Staging is a strategy for marketing your house, not decorating it. Once you're finished all the staging steps, you'll see that even though your house is less "you," it will be more appealing to a greater number of people.

Nine Good Reasons to De-clutter and Depersonalize

Need more reasons to conquer the clutter and put away your personal stuff? Reducing the number of items left out and depersonalizing an area achieves the following:

1. **Increases space**. Too many belongings in a room make it feel cramped and small. Buyers want homes that feel light and spacious. Removing as many items as possible will add prime living space.
2. **Creates more storage**. Cluttered shelves, cupboards, and closets are major buyer deterrents. Storage sells, so make the most of your storage space by clearing it out and organizing it.
3. **Showcases the home's best features**. Removing distracting clutter and personal items allows buyers to notice the features of the house. For example, buyers won't fully appreciate a new tub surround if they're busy looking at the bath toys in the tub and the beach towels draped over the shower rod.
4. **Encourages buyers to imagine their own possessions in the home**. A home filled with personal belongings gives buyers the sense that they are intruding on your space, so they will be less inclined to imagine themselves living in your home and thus less likely to assume "virtual ownership" and to buy it.
5. **Creates a neat, fresh, and inviting environment**. A cluttered room looks confusing and makes people feel overwhelmed, distracted, and stressed. A clean and organized room creates a sense of calm and is a haven from stress.
6. **Shows that your home is loved and well maintained**. If buyers see messy piles of clutter lying about, they might assume that the seller didn't bother taking care of other, more important details. A tidy and organized house sends the message that you are meticulous with home upkeep.

7. **Makes completing the other staging steps much easier**. It's difficult to complete repairs, upgrades, cleaning, and styling when the house is cluttered. Clearing out the clutter will make cleaning and styling much easier.

8. **Prepares you for moving.** Less stuff means fewer boxes and a less costly move. By packing and storing items that you won't need during the selling process, you'll have less packing and sorting to do once your home sells and you are ready to relocate.

9. **Makes moving in easier.** Making decisions now about what to keep and what to purge means that when you move into your new place all you'll have to do is unpack. Precious space in your new home won't immediately be filled with items you don't need or want.

The Home Staging Definition of "Clutter"

The word "clutter" usually brings to mind a disorganized mess—piles of laundry and dishes, toys lying everywhere, and mail and papers strewn about. For the purposes of home staging, however, clutter includes not only these obvious examples but also anything else that takes up space unnecessarily or is highly personal.

Valued and beautiful possessions, therefore, can be visual clutter if they make the room seem smaller or are blocking a path, view, or important selling point. For example, a pile of books in front of a cupboard, a bread maker on a small kitchen counter, and plants in front of a window are all clutter even though they are useful items that you will want to use in your new house.

Every item in a staged room should fulfill at least one of the following criteria:

- It is used frequently,
- It highlights the purpose of the room, or
- It makes the room look appealing.

Remove anything that you won't absolutely need to use in the next few months or that doesn't enhance the look of the room. By this guideline, a lot of stuff should be removed. For example, you'll need some dishes and cutlery, but you won't need all 10 place settings. You'll need linens, but not extra sheets for every bed in the house. You also won't need all your photo albums, music, or books. And depending on the season, you may be able to remove three seasons of clothing for everyone in the house.

If you're short on time, you can simply pack everything and store it until you move. However, we highly recommend you pare down your possessions now. It costs money to store and move boxes, so it makes sense to get rid of items that you don't want or need now so you won't have to move them and deal with them again later.

Although everything in this laundry room is useful, leaving it all out makes the room look cluttered and confined.

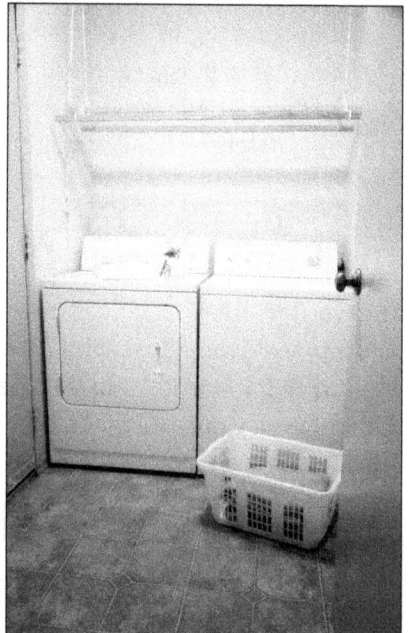

Simply putting the laundry away and storing the remaining supplies out of sight makes the room serene and spacious.

Although packing items before you move may seem like a lot of work, you'll have to eventually pack them anyway. Packing and storing items not needed before the move is an essential part of staging; it will significantly increase the free space in your home and thus increase your home's perceived value.

Storing Your Stuff

So where, exactly, are you supposed to store all your stuff once it's packed?

Ideally, store your boxes off-site, either at a friend or relative's house or in a rented storage unit. Removing all the boxes will make the house roomier and hide tell-tale evidence that it has been staged.

Another option is to rent a portable moving and storage unit. The company delivers the unit right to your house, and after you fill it, they take it away for off-site storage. This arrangement is perfect for staging purposes.

If you absolutely can't store your boxes off-site, stack them neatly in a shed, the garage, or a corner of the basement. Stack them (safely) in tall piles to leave as much of the floor visible as possible. If necessary, install extra shelving to get the boxes off the floor.

Whatever you do, do not stack your boxes in main living areas, not even in closets or shelving units. Storage space helps sell a house, so don't fill it up unnecessarily.

Typical Clutter Found in Most Homes (and What to Do with It)

All types of items can become clutter, but in general, common sources of clutter in most homes tend to be the following:

- **Papers.** Even with the Internet and email, there always seems to be too many papers cluttering most homes. Newspapers, flyers, receipts, take-out menus, school newsletters and homework: the list of papers that comes into the house seems endless. Recycle as much paper as possible, and gather together all papers that need immediate action, such as unpaid bills. Keep these neatly contained in one place (such as in a tray on a desk or near the phone), and then deal with them as soon as possible. Organize papers that you need or want to keep for the long term, such as important receipts, paid bills, or magazine clippings. Sort these papers into labeled file folders and store them out of sight.

- **Children's toys.** Toys often clutter family homes. Some of the biggest offenders are collectible toys, such as die-cast cars, dolls, and stuffed animals. Pare down your kids' toys to only a select few that they use most often, and pack away the rest. Reassure younger children that their toys will be waiting for them after you move. Show them the boxes of their packed toys, and label these boxes with their names and the message, "For our new house." Another option is to store some of the extra toys at a relative or friend's house. You can drop by to exchange toys or have your kids play with them there.

- **Items that don't fit with the intended purpose of the room.** Examples include a television in a bedroom, exercise equipment in the living room, or toys in the dining room. Even though your family may use those items where they are, they distract buyers from focusing on the room, and they may confuse buyers about the room's purpose. If the item wouldn't be in a show home's living room, it shouldn't be in your staged living room.

- **Collections.** People love to display collections, but large collections of items are distracting. When staging your house, remove and pack your collections. This includes anything from beautiful paintings to hand-carved duck decoys to Royal Doulton figurines. However, set aside a few items that you might use later when styling the house.

- **Small accessories.** When it comes to accessories, less is more and bigger is better. Fewer, larger accessories have a bigger impact and create less clutter than many smaller accessories. Therefore, for staging purposes, pack away accessories that are roughly smaller than a soft ball.

- **Excess or large furniture.** Extra furniture and furniture that is too large for the room also clutter a room. Clear out a piece or two to maximize the floor space, create a clear pathway through the room, and increase the feeling of spaciousness. Aim for a minimalist look. For example, in the dining room, keep only the table (remove extensions, if possible), two to four chairs, and a sideboard or china cabinet. In an average-sized living room with a fireplace and built-in cabinets, keep only a sofa, two chairs (or a love seat), a coffee table, and two end tables. Smaller rooms can do without the coffee table. Larger rooms can also include one more piece of furniture, such as a piano, sofa table, or bookcase. In a bedroom, limit furniture to the bed, one or two bedside tables, and a dresser. Removing the extra dresser makes the bedroom seem larger and also sends the message that you have plenty of closet space. (If you don't have lots of closet space, de-cluttering will help). Hallways are usually narrow spaces and should not have any furniture in them.

- **Craft Supplies.** Many creative people enjoy sewing, scrapbooking, quilting, or other types of crafts or hobbies. Craft projects usually require a lot of space and often the materials are left out in the open, especially if the project is ongoing. When selling your house, you'll simply have to put your hobbies and projects on hold and pack them away until you move. Get some boxes or large plastic totes and store everything in them so it's all contained together. This will allow you to reclaim the room and showcase the space, not your projects.

- **Cleaning supplies.** Of course you need soaps, detergents, mops, brooms, sponges, a vacuum cleaner, and so on. Just make sure to store them where buyers can't see them; for example, don't leave a toilet brush in the bathroom or a dish drainer on the kitchen counter. Why remind buyers of work? Also don't cram cleaning supplies on an open shelf or into a closet, ready to fall on anyone who opens the door. If you need to store them on an open shelf, contain them in plastic totes or attractive baskets.

- **Pet Paraphernalia.** We love our pets, but potential buyers may not. Remove all evidence of your pet, especially for showings. That means moving the kennel or cat condo out of sight and putting away pet toys, leashes, dishes, and food. If you need to keep some items handy, contain them in a basket stored in a closet.

- **Anything that has not been used in the last six to twelve months.** These might include clothing that's out of style or the wrong size, obsolete items like videotapes or audiocassettes (maybe even DVDs and CDs), broken items, exercise equipment, and unfinished projects. Most of us keep some items that we never use out of guilt or a sense of obligation, such as impractical (but thoughtful) gifts or expensive impulse buys that we later regretted. Once you recognize the emotions tied in with these items, it is easier to let them go. However, whether you decide to ditch these unused items or hang on to them, store them out of sight to add more space to your home.

Clutter Hotspots

Some of the most important areas of a house also seem to be the places that attract the most clutter. Pay particular attention to the following clutter hotspots:

- **Kitchen and Bathroom Counters.** Kitchens and bathrooms are a top priority for buyers, and the most visible spaces in these rooms are the countertops. Remove everything from countertops except for up to three decorative items. That means that the kitchen counter should not be home to small appliances (toaster, blender, coffee pot, slow cooker, etc.), cereal boxes, canisters, spice racks, utensils, and so on. Only leave out an attractive appliance for staging purposes, such as a high-end coffee maker. Sort through your kitchen items and decide what you will use in the next few months and what can be packed away. Keep items that are staying in the cabinets or drawers. Also clear the bathroom counter, removing items such as toothbrushes, lotions, razors, makeup, and your hair dryer. Now's your chance to get rid of expired or unused toiletries and cosmetics. (Bring expired medications to a pharmacy for safe disposal.) Again, keep remaining items in a cabinet or drawer so that they are out of sight.

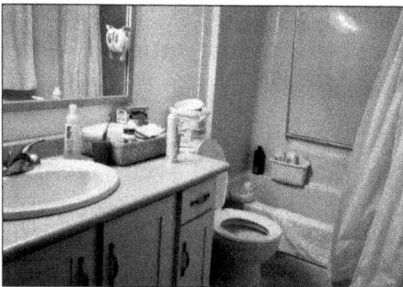

With personal items left out, this cluttered bathroom counter makes the whole room seem cramped and confused.

Packing away the personal items on the counter and in the shower makes the bathroom tidy and organized.

■ **Closets, Bookshelves, and Cabinets.** Storage space is a valuable feature; potential buyers want to see lots of it. If a closet, bookshelf, or built-in cabinet is full, reduce the number of items by one-third to one-half. In other words, shelves, closets, and cabinets should be only one-half to two-thirds full. Follow a "Nothing up top" rule: Leave nothing on top of cabinets, and empty the top shelves in cabinets and closets. Also leave the floor space totally clear. Although this sounds extreme, it will send the message that you have ample storage space. It also reduces distractions, allowing buyers to have a good view of the space. If you must use the top shelves or floor space, contain all the items in a basket or two. An average closet takes about one to two hours to de-clutter. Plan to give yourself plenty of time to get the job done.

See the difference made by packing away out-of-season coats and shoes, adding a shoe organizer, and clearing off the top shelf? Extra hats and mitts are stored in the basket on the top shelf.

Bedrooms. Bedrooms are another area that is often cluttered and busy. Buyers want to see bedrooms that look inviting and relaxing. De-cluttering will help to make your bedroom feel like a retreat. Start by clearing all items from the tops of dressers and bedside tables, leaving only a lamp and a clock. To make life easier, store your usual bedside materials (books, reading glasses, etc.) in a plastic tote and slide it under the bed. Remove items that don't usually belong in bedrooms, such as a treadmill or TV (sorry, but TVs don't say "retreat"). In children's rooms, contain toys in a bin in a corner of the room. Remove or put away all stuffed toys except for two or three for show. If a desk must remain, make sure it's neat and tidy. Also make children's rooms as gender- and age-neutral as possible (e.g., take down themed décor and remove posters). Remove everything on the door as well, including stickers, nameplates, and doorknob hangers.

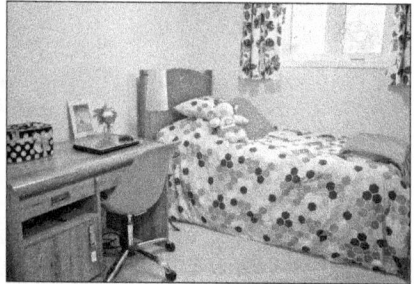

Before and after de-cluttering a pre-teen's room. Notice that the desk had to stay, but removing the hutch and printer made the room much more spacious.

Home Office. A home office can be a busy place and can easily become overwhelmed with office supplies and work projects. Show potential buyers that your home office is a functional workspace by organizing it to make it seem more spacious. Begin by clearing off the desk and only replacing items that are essential and need to be within reach. Keep in mind that if you work on a computer, you might not need a jar of pens and pencils on your desk. Can you live without your printer or fax machine before the move? Ideally, have only a computer, monitor, and mouse at your workstation. Store extra paper, books, and other supplies in a closed cupboard or drawer, if possible. If you must keep confidential papers or files in your office while the house is for sale, make sure to keep them out of sight. People are curious, and anything left out will probably be examined. If you're short on storage, and if you have space, consider adding a file cabinet or closed bookshelf. Lidded boxes and baskets are also great for storage. If you can, remove any large binders off the bookshelf, or try to store them out of sight for a more streamlined look (see Chapter 6 for hints on styling bookshelves). Finally, try to limit the number of cords and wires showing. Consider replacing some devices with wireless or Bluetooth versions (such as the keyboard or mouse). You can also purchase inexpensive cord clips or cable wraps to bundle your cords neatly together.

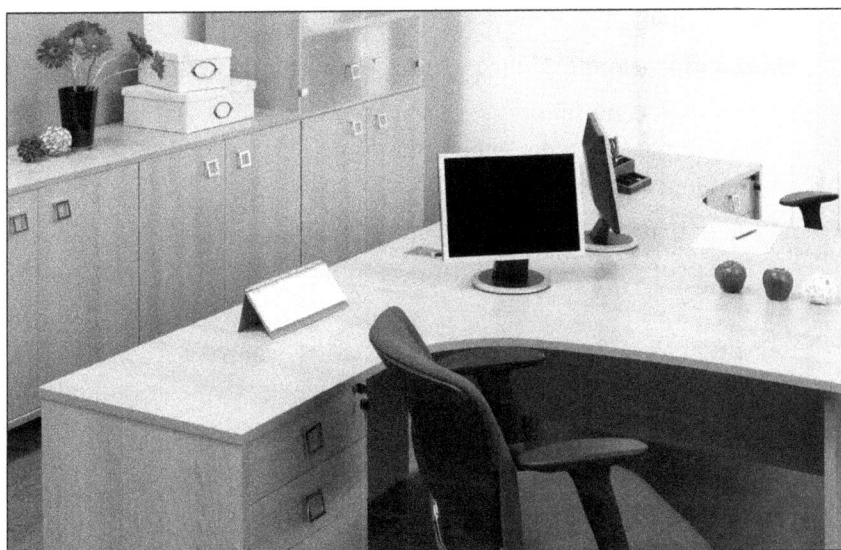

In this tidy home office, the desk and shelving are clear of books, binders, and extra supplies. The decorative accessories are a nice touch, and notice how the attractive filing boxes are used for extra storage.

Identifying Personal Items

Identifying items that are personal in nature can be tricky. In general, if your picture or name is on an item, it is too personal. If it conveys some of your religious or political beliefs, it is too personal. And if it represents a highly specific, quirky, or unique taste, it's too personal.

The following are examples of items to pack away in order to depersonalize your home:

- Family photos.
- Framed degrees, diplomas, or certificates.
- Awards and trophies.
- Collections.
- Bills and personal correspondence.
- Calendars with notes and appointments written on the dates.
- Children's artwork.
- Religious items.
- Books or magazines with controversial or political-themed titles.
- Medications, especially with your name on the label. (If these can't be packed away, store them out of sight when photographing or showing your home.)
- Anything that might cause a negative reaction, such as ashtrays, artwork showing nudity, taxidermy or mounted deer antlers, hunting guns.
- Items that make your home uniquely yours, such as garden gnomes, an African mask collection from your travels, or homemade quilts on display on the wall.

Personalized Rooms

People often personalize their homes by using a room in a different way than it was intended. For example, a spare bedroom could be used as a craft room, or the living room could be changed into a dining room. Buyers need to see the rooms and spaces as they were intended. What worked well for you may not work for another family and may instead create confusion in the minds of the people viewing your home. Therefore, whenever possible revert each room back to its intended function.

A bedroom converted to an office, however, may not need to change, depending on the type of buyer you expect to be interested in the house. If you think mainly families with children will be viewing the house, then consider changing it back to a bedroom. Otherwise, leaving it as an office should be fine. Ask your real estate agent for advice.

Do not use a spare bedroom as a storage area. Show as much square footage of livable space as you can.

Tips for Tackling Clutter

Once you identify the clutter and personal items in your home, you need a plan for getting rid of them. You have four options for dealing with these items, which can be summarized using the acronym **PAST**:

- **P**ack (and store until you move),
- Give **A**way (e.g., donate to a charity, list on Freecycle.org, or give to friends),
- **S**ell (at a garage sale, a consignment store, or through a website such as Kijiji or Craigslist), or
- **T**rash (or recycle, whenever possible).

Pack only the items that you intend to move to your next home. Give away, sell, or trash/recycle the rest, as appropriate. For example, donate your kids' outgrown clothing to the Salvation Army, sell the old desk on Kijiji, send the broken lamp to the trash, and recycle the piles of old magazines and outdated coupons. Voila! Gone are the items that you don't need in your home during the selling process, and gone are the items that you don't want to haul to your next home.

If you need help deciding what to do with an item, use the De-cluttering Decision Tree included in the appendix.

Although de-cluttering is physically and emotionally draining, it is absolutely essential for proper staging. Review the section on self-motivation in Chapter 2, if necessary, and get to work. The following are general principles and tips to help you through the process.

Think Twice about Selling Your Stuff

Selling items that you no longer need is a good way to rid your home of clutter. However, unless you can simply haul your stuff to a consignment store, most other methods of selling your goods involve effort and time. Hosting a garage sale takes many days to sort, price, and organize the items and at least a full day of selling. Even selling your items online can take days or weeks and involves taking pictures, posting the ads, communicating with buyers, and arranging for pickup or delivery. All the while, the items you want to sell are still stored in your house. If you don't have much time before listing your house, consider giving away some of these items instead of selling them. You will be helping others and speeding up this step. You may also be able to deduct the value of your charitable donations from your income tax.

Be Prepared

- **Plan to start early**. Don't wait until your list date is looming before you begin. If you allow yourself time, you'll feel calmer and won't become overwhelmed or exhausted by the job. Don't expect to finish the whole house in one day. Plan to spend at least a few hours in each room; basements and garages usually take longer.

- **Begin when the room or area is reasonably clean and tidy.** Don't make the job harder by having to work around extra mess. For example, wash and put away the dishes before tackling the kitchen counters.

- **Gather the following supplies:**
  - Boxes (preferably the same size so they stack well)
  - Large, durable plastic garbage bags
  - Packing paper and tape
  - Markers

- **Enlist help.** Have family members help out. Don't expect young children to be able to do this independently, however. Ask older kids to sort through their own rooms, and then review their work. Ask friends to pitch in. It's useful to have someone who isn't emotionally attached to your things help you decide what should go. They can also help with packing and moving boxes.

Get to Work

- **Organize the storage area first.** If you must store your boxes in the garage or basement, clear out the area where you plan to stack your boxes and leave the rest of the room for later. Don't try to de-clutter the entire room now because storage areas are usually the most challenging to organize.

- **Once your storage area is ready, start work in the smallest and/ or least cluttered room**. If time is short and you are about to list your home, start with the areas that will be viewed first, with a special emphasis on the kitchen and main living area.

- **Break the work into steps**. Focus on one room or area at a time. Start small so as not to be overwhelmed. Work on one shelf, drawer, or cupboard at a time. Finish one area before moving on to another. Gaining a sense of completion will energize and motivate you as you move to more cluttered areas.

- **Establish a system.** Get out your boxes and plastic bags. You'll need four plastic bags at all times; label each one either "Trash," "Recycle" (for papers, magazines, cardboard, etc.), "Give Away" (for donations), or "Sell" (for items to sell later). Take out a box for items that you will pack and move to your new place, and a box for items that you're not sure about; label this box "Maybe." As the bags and boxes fill up, move them out of the room and replace them with new ones.

- **Start at the doorway and move around the room**. Begin at the tops of shelves and work your way down. Start in the corners of closets and work towards the middle. Begin with the parts of the room you can immediately see (e.g., countertops, shelves) and then move to closed storage areas (e.g., cupboards, drawers).

- **Focusing on one area, remove every item**. For each item, ask yourself whether you will need to use it before selling the house. If the answer is "yes," set it aside in a "Keep" pile; you will find a place for it after you're finished in this area. If the answer is "no," decide whether you want to pack, give away, sell, or trash (or recycle) it. Remember to pack all personal items such as family photos and diplomas.

- **Make quick decisions.** Take no more than 5 to 10 seconds to make a decision. The longer you take, the more likely you'll hang onto something you don't really need or want.

- **If you can't decide whether to pack, give away, sell, or trash an item, place it in the "Maybe" box.** You can go back to it when you're finished and decide then. Be careful about the "Maybe" box. Don't use it as an excuse to avoid making decisions. Too many items in this box will derail the process. Aim for allowing no more than 5 percent of your items in the "Maybe" box.

- **Don't second-guess yourself.** Trust your decisions and resist the temptation to dig through the bags to retrieve things.

- **Don't lose momentum.** However tempted you are to leaf through old photo albums and memorabilia, this isn't the time for nostalgia. Keep focused on the task.

- **Clear all horizontal surfaces, and work your way through shelves, drawers, cupboards, and closets.** Buyers will be checking out all storage spaces.

- **Get a start on your cleaning by wiping down the empty surface** as you clear out shelves and cupboards.

- **Keep some items to use later when styling your rooms**. Don't get carried away and pack or get rid of everything. You don't want your home to feel empty and cold. Set aside 1, 3, or 5 of your favorite pieces from a collection and pack the rest. Choose some accessories that you think you may use to style the room later (e.g., art, vases, plants, candles). You don't have to decide now; just set them aside in a box and you can figure out what you'll use when you style the house (see Chapter 6).

- **Label each box after it's filled.** On the box top, label where it belongs (e.g, "master bedroom"), and on its side list the contents (e.g., "queen sheets, two pillows").

- **Expect that each space will look worse before it looks better**. As you pull your rooms apart, things may feel chaotic. Persevere and you'll see that calmness will return.

- **Focus on your progress instead of the amount of work left to be done.** Remind yourself that you're doing this to make your house sell quicker and for more money and to make moving day easier. Notice how much lighter you and your home feel as you eliminate all the extraneous stuff.

Finish the Job

Once you finish de-cluttering the room, put all items in the "Keep" pile back where they belong. Some items may belong in another room. If you don't have a place for each item or if there are too many items and the area is still looking cluttered, reassess whether you really need them. Remember, pack or get rid of items that are not absolutely necessary.

Deal with the boxes and bags immediately:

- Move the packed and labeled boxes to your storage area. Make sure they are stacked neatly and out of the way. If you are storing them off-site, set them aside neatly until you are ready to bring them to the storage unit.

- In many cities, you can arrange for local charities to pick up donations. If you post on Freecycle, you can arrange with the person who wants your items to pick them up at your doorstep. Consider hiring a hauling service to pick up trash and donations. If you must deliver your donations yourself, put the boxes in your car so they're out of the house and ready to be dropped off the next time you're out.

- Take another look in the "Maybe" box(es). You will likely have greater clarity this second time and will be able to decide what to do with these items. If you're still not sure about some items, pack them and deal with them after you move. Simply seal the box and label its contents. When you move into your new home, set the "Maybe" boxes aside for six more months. If after this period you haven't missed anything or had to open the box to get out any of the contents, then you can bring the entire box, still sealed, to a charity.

Don't undo your hard work by allowing new clutter to creep in. Chapter 9 includes tips on keeping your home tidy and organized while it is on the market.

If you don't have the time, patience, energy, or interest to thoroughly de-clutter, consider hiring a staging company to help with this essential step.

De-cluttering/Depersonalizing CHECKLIST

Front Entrance

❑ Remove furniture that's too large for the space (e.g., if it blocks the traffic flow).

❑ Reduce items in the closets at the front and back doors: remove out-of-season coats and footwear, and clear off the top shelf. If you must use the top shelf, store items in baskets or bins.

❑ Store all shoes and coats in the closet, especially when photographing and showing the house. Place a shoe rack in the closet for efficient storage.

❑ Move key and coat hooks out of sight.

Kitchen

❑ Clear the windowsill.

❑ Remove the throw rug.

❑ Remove anything containing personal information, such as bills, day planners, calendars, etc. Store these in a drawer or file, out of sight.

❑ Remove items that wouldn't be seen in a kitchen showroom, such the phone book, a TV, pet dishes, recycling bins, or a garbage can. Find new places for these items, out of sight.

❑ Clear the countertops, removing appliances, canisters, utensils, the dish rack, etc. Pack items that you don't need in the short term, and keep needed items under the counters or in drawers.

Cabinets:

❑ Remove items stored on top of cabinets (e.g., decorative greenery and vases). Dust cabinet tops.

❑ Empty each cabinet, and clean the interior with warm, soapy water.

❑ Replace only the items you will use before the move. Leave one-third to one-half of the shelves empty.

❑ Leave the top shelf bare.

❑ In the cabinet under the sink, reduce contents and organize remaining items into baskets or plastic bins.

Drawers:

- ☐ Empty kitchen drawers and wipe down the inside.
- ☐ Replace only the items you will use before the move. Remove extra cutlery, specialty gadgets, or multiples of the same items.
- ☐ Replace remaining items neatly, using silverware holders and drawer dividers.

Pantry:

- ☐ Remove everything and clean the shelves with warm, soapy water.
- ☐ Throw out expired goods and pack or donate non-expired goods that you won't use before you move.
- ☐ Replace only the items you will use before the move. Leave one-third to one-half of the pantry empty. Keep the top shelf bare.
- ☐ Store bulk food items (flour, sugar, rice) in airtight, see-through canisters or in neatly labeled plastic containers.
- ☐ Store small, loose items (e.g., seasoning mixes, packaged soup) in a clear plastic container without a lid.
- ☐ Group like items together (e.g., canned goods in one area and rice and grains in another).
- ☐ Place taller items at the back of shelves and shorter items near the front.
- ☐ Line a shelf or two with matching containers for a neat, organized appearance.
- ☐ Turn canned goods so the labels face outward.
- ☐ Store larger items on the lower shelves and smaller items on the centre and upper shelves.
- ☐ Store only food in the pantry; keeping other items here suggests a lack of storage space.
- ☐ Clear the pantry floor. If you must use this space, store items in lidded baskets or bins.

Refrigerator:

- ☐ Clear the top of the refrigerator.

- ☐ Remove everything from the front and sides of the refrigerator, including magnets, photos, menus, notes, children's artwork, etc.
- ☐ De-clutter inside the refrigerator (removing unused condiments, clearing out empty jars, etc.).

Dining Room

- ☐ Remove table extensions. (If you need them, leave them for now but remove before taking pictures or showing the house.)
- ☐ Remove excess furniture. Keep only the table, 2 to 4 chairs (unless you need more chairs or the table is very large), and a sideboard or china cabinet.
- ☐ Remove furniture that is too large for the room. For example, if you have a buffet and hutch, consider removing the hutch.
- ☐ Remove excess and unhealthy plants.
- ☐ Reduce items inside china cabinet to a few key pieces.
- ☐ Reduce the number of accessories in the room.

Main Living Areas
(Living Room, Family Room, or Great Room)

- ☐ Remove items that would not be seen in a show room, such as toys or exercise equipment.
- ☐ Pack and store collections, family photographs, diplomas, and anything with your name or picture on it.
- ☐ Remove excess furniture and furniture too large for the space.
- ☐ Remove excess and unhealthy plants.
- ☐ Remove throw rugs (keep large area rug).
- ☐ Reduce the number of electronics in the room and tuck away cords.
- ☐ Remove anything blocking windows or doorways.
- ☐ Remove art or photos on narrow walls (i.e., walls less than 2 feet wide).
- ☐ Remove some accessories and wall art. (Set aside to possibly use later when styling the room.) Leave at least one empty wall.

☐ Reduce items on shelves until they are only one-half to two-thirds full.

Bathrooms

☐ Remove fuzzy toilet seat cover and matching mat.

☐ Remove some accessories and wall art. (Set aside for later.)

Vanity top:

☐ Clear the countertop, removing toothbrushes, soaps and lotions, shavers, makeup, hair dryer, curling iron, etc.

☐ Keep items that you use daily or frequently in drawers or a cabinet. Pack or discard/recycle the rest.

Cabinets and drawers:

☐ Empty drawers and cabinets. Wipe down the interior.

☐ Replace only the items that you will use before you move. Pack or discard the rest.

☐ Organize small items (e.g., nail clippers, nail polish, hair elastics) in zippered cosmetic cases, and larger items (e.g., cosmetics) in baskets or bins.

Tub/Shower:

☐ Remove tub toys and store them in a cabinet.

☐ Remove extra bottles and soaps from the shower.

Bedrooms

☐ Remove extra furniture (e.g., bookcases, extra dressers.) Unless the room is very large, limit furniture to the bed, one or two bedside tables, and a dresser.

☐ Remove anything that doesn't normally belong in a bedroom, such as a TV, treadmill, or computer desk.

☐ Clear the tops of the dresser and bedside tables.

☐ Remove personal items such as jewelry, lotions, papers, medications, etc.

☐ Remove back-of-door hooks or hangers (these suggest a lack of storage space).

- ☐ Reduce contents of the closet until it is only one-half to two-thirds full. Pack away as many clothes and shoes as possible. Clear the top shelf, and remove items from the closet floor (leave only neatly paired shoes, if necessary). Group like items together (e.g., hang all shirts together, all pants together, etc.). Hang like items from lightest to darkest colour.
- ☐ Remove some accessories and wall art (set aside for later).
- ☐ In children's rooms, contain toys in a bin placed in a corner of the room. Take down themed décor and posters. Remove stickers, plaques, and name plates on the door.

Home Office

- ☐ Clear off your desk, leaving only the essentials.
- ☐ Sort through papers, discarding what you can and storing the remainder in files or folders.
- ☐ Store infrequently used items in containers or boxes.
- ☐ If you need extra storage, and if there's space, add a filing cabinet or bookcase.
- ☐ Take down framed diplomas, certificates, and family photos.
- ☐ Remove equipment that rarely is used (e.g., fax machine, paper cutter).
- ☐ Reduce wires; consider replacing some devices with wireless or Bluetooth versions (such as the keyboard or mouse).
- ☐ Use a wire management system (e.g., cord clips, cable wraps, etc.) to contain cables and wires.
- ☐ Remove some wall art, if necessary.
- ☐ Remove extra furniture (e.g., extra chairs or tables).
- ☐ Reduce number of items on the bookshelves until the shelves are only one-half to two-thirds full.

Hallways and Stairwells

❑ Remove furniture.

❑ Keep all items off the stairs.

❑ Remove throw rugs.

❑ Remove all pictures and artwork from walls.

Laundry Room

❑ Remove detergents and other products that aren't used routinely.

❑ Store products neatly in a closed cupboard. If you don't have a cupboard, contain these items in baskets or bins and store them on a shelf.

❑ Store the ironing board and clothes drying rack out of sight.

Linen Closet

❑ Sort through your linens. Leave only two or three towels per person in the household. Leave only one set of sheets for each adult bed and two sets for each child's bed. Pack away the rest.

❑ Fold linens neatly (fold side facing out) and stack in piles (towels with towels, sheets with sheets).

❑ Use the "hotel" fold for all towels and stack like colours together.

❑ Keep lighter coloured items together on upper shelves and darker coloured items on lower shelves.

❑ Stack folded, matching hand towels on top of matching bath towels.

❑ Stack neatly folded sheets with matching, folded pillowcases on top.

❑ Slip a fresh smelling bar of soap between stacks of sheets or towels to give your closet a fresh smell.

❑ Take toilet paper out of plastic wrapping and stack neatly in a wicker basket on the bottom shelf.

❑ If necessary, store an extra duvet, quilt, or pillow on the top shelf; otherwise, keep this shelf clear of items.

Back Entrance

❑ Make sure items left out are neatly stored (e.g., line up boots or shoes up on a mat).

❑ If you have coat hooks, make sure each holds only one coat.

❑ Move the recycling bins and sports equipment into the garage, if possible. If not possible, bring in your recyclables regularly and contain the sports equipment neatly in a bag.

Basement/Garage

❑ Clear out as many items as possible.

❑ Store remaining items in a neat, organized manner. Put similar items together. For example, all store garden implements together in one area, and tools in another.

❑ Use large storage bins to keep organized. Having fewer, larger bins or boxes is neater and less cluttered than many smaller ones. Label the bins and order them on a shelf.

❑ Use hooks and shelves to store items off the floor.

❑ In the garage, clear the area around the door so buyers can easily step out.

❑ Make sure there's enough room to park a car in the garage.

chapter four

Step 2: Repairing and Upgrading

HOMEBUYERS ARE NOTORIOUSLY CAUTIOUS. When they walk through a house or view it online, they are looking for flaws. Although they might *want* to love a house, they're really there to uncover reasons to *not* love it. They are looking with a critical eye, searching for any signs of problems or neglect.

Many sellers choose to ignore outdated details in the house and put off doing minor repairs, thinking they aren't that important. Or they decide to put the house on the market "as is" and see what happens. Both are big mistakes. Easily fixed problems like wallpaper, bold paint colours, worn out flooring, leaking faucets, and dated light fixtures can become deal breakers because they practically scream "too much work." They also send powerful messages: this home has not been fastidiously maintained, and bigger problems—and big expenses—could be coming.

According to a survey by Coldwell Banker Associates, only a small minority of homebuyers (7%) is willing to purchase a "fixer-upper"; the vast majority (more than 80%) wants a home that's move-in ready. They don't want to invest time, money, or effort fixing problems. And they certainly don't want to discover costly surprises after they move in.

The second step to staging your home is to complete needed repairs and upgrades. Focus on doing repairs and upgrades that will improve the appearance, safety, or function of the home. Even the smallest improvements can help a house sell faster and for more money.

This is not so much a "how-to" chapter as it is a "what-to" chapter. There are many resources online and in print that will give you step-by-step instructions for carrying out home repairs and improvements. This chapter outlines the most common problems that should be repaired before the house is listed; it also describes the upgrades that homebuyers want and that usually provide the best return on investment.

Repairs

When we talk about small repairs, we mean minor issues like broken doorbells or squeaky doors: those pesky little problems that always crop up but that we often ignore, adapt to, or even forget. Of course, when selling your house you need to attend to all major repairs (like a furnace or water heater that doesn't work) or fully disclose unresolved issues.

The good news is you don't need to invest a lot of money in repairs to realize a significant return. For example, a survey by the blog HomeGain in 2010 estimated the cost of completing plumbing repairs before listing a house (such as repairing leaky faucets and repairing caulk or grout around tub and tile areas) to be about $300 and the return on the investment to be about $1000. That's a 330% return on your investment!

Identifying Needed Repairs

It is important to identify needed repairs before potential buyers do. You probably already know about many of the repairs requiring attention in your home. Now is the time to finally deal with them.

The checklist at the end of this chapter lists the most common types of repairs needed in most homes. Bring the checklist with you as you go through each room or area of your house, and note all problems.

You may not have time to attend to everything on your list, but do as much as you can within your timeframe and budget. Tackle the most obvious problems first and then move on to the less noticeable ones. Also begin working in the areas that buyers will look at first: the front exterior and yard (see Chapter 7), the front entrance, and then on to the kitchen/dining areas, main living areas, bathrooms, and bedrooms.

DIY or SOS?

You need to decide whether you have the time and know-how to complete repair projects yourself. There are many books and online resources to help you through each step of whatever job you take on. However, it's always best to hire a licensed trade professional for repairs that are beyond your abilities, unsafe for you to do (e.g., roof repair), or that involve a major mechanical system (e.g., plumbing or electrical). It's very important to get the job done right and in a timely manner. Sometimes trying to tackle a tricky job on your own ends up costing more in terms of money, time, and mistakes. Ask at a home improvement store for referrals when looking for a licensed trade professional.

Pre-Sale Home Inspection

Although buyers usually arrange for a professional home inspection before finalizing the sale, some home sellers are now choosing to arrange for professional inspections before they list.

Mike Holmes, Canada's home inspection and repairs guru, suggests there are several advantages to having a professional pre-sale inspection:

- It will reveal any problems so you can avoid costly last-minute surprises.

- It will establish the true condition of your house, enabling you to set a realistic asking price.

- It will provide you a checklist of needed repairs, which will help you to prioritize.

- It will strengthen your position when it comes time to negotiate. Buyers usually over-estimate the cost of home improvements. If they hire a home inspector and find out that the roof needs to be repaired, for example, they may either withdraw or drastically reduce their offer. Usually the price reduction is far more than the average cost of repairs. However, if you know ahead of time about the roof, you can either fix the problem yourself and shop around for the best price, or you can disclose the issue to the buyer and be prepared by offering a reasonable discount to cover the cost of the repair (after getting an estimate from a professional).

Arranging for a pre-sale inspection is not a common practice, but it may give you a distinct advantage over your competition. You can show potential buyers your inspection report and indicate the work completed, demonstrating that you are upfront and committed to selling a quality product.

Upgrades

After taking care of repairs, you can now focus on upgrades.

Major renovations are not part of the staging process. Staging mainly involves using what you already have to present your home in the best possible light. Nevertheless, many homebuyers recognize that upgrading certain features will increase their selling price.

Several relatively inexpensive improvements will boost the value of your home and make it stand out from the competition. Although you probably already have in mind upgrades you'd like to do, you may need to set these aside and instead focus on upgrades that the majority of buyers will want.

A recent Royal LePage survey identified upgrades most popular among buyers, and found the following:

- 79% of buyers want renovated kitchens
- 73% want renovated bathrooms
- 62% want new flooring
- 36% want updated décor

Be careful to not start too many renovation projects. The cost and time involved can quickly get out of hand, and if you do too much you may not recoup your expenses.

Visit the Appraisal Institute of Canada website (aicanada.ca) to view an interactive guide that calculates the average expected return for specific renovations. The return on investment (ROI) is the percentage of your investment that you can expect to get back in excess of the original investment. For example, a 50% ROI means that you can expect to get back what you put in plus 50% more. Box 4.1 lists the renovation projects with the best ROI according to the Appraisal Institute of Canada.

Box 4.1 *Renovations with Best Return on Investment*

Renovation Project	Approximate ROI
Kitchen renovation	75-100%
Bathroom renovation	75-100%
Replace knobs and hardware	75-100%
Paint (exterior or interior)	50-100%
Install new light fixtures	60-70%
Flooring upgrade	50-75%
Window/door replacement	50-75%

Source: Appraisal Institute of Canada RENOVA, Royal LePage, 2011.

Keep in mind that to get full return on your investment, upgrades must be in line with the standards of your neighbourhood. For instance, if your house is in a moderate neighbourhood, buyers will expect a moderately priced home and will not want to pay for luxury upgrades. On the other hand, if you are surrounded by high-end homes, then luxury details such as hardwood floors and granite countertops are probably expected. Before proceeding with a costly project, talk with a real estate agent about which renovations would be most profitable considering the local market and the condition, age, and location of your home.

Houses that are well out of date and haven't been maintained may require an investment that won't bring a full return. If this is the case with your house, you'll need to price your house accordingly and perhaps expect more time to sell. (The other staging steps—de-cluttering, cleaning, and styling—will still help sell the house, and are even more important now.) If only certain areas of your house are in poor condition, however, you may decide that extensive work in these areas will help it sell more quickly. Talk to your real estate agent.

As with repairs, you may be able to complete many of the upgrades listed in this chapter yourself. However, make sure you know when to call in a professional. The Appraisal Institute of Canada warns that substandard work on upgrades may actually *decrease* the value of your home.

If you are planning to list your home immediately, consider some of the simple lower-cost, high-impact upgrades discussed below and listed in the checklist at the end of this chapter. Consider these suggestions as a "wish list" from which to pick and choose those that are most important for your house. The cumulative effect of repairs and upgrades can be dramatic.

Upgrading with Style

When you're investing the time, effort, and money into upgrades, it's important to choose styles that are current and popular. You don't have to be a cutting-edge hipster (in fact, we strongly discourage it), but in order to appeal to the masses, your choice of upgrades should reflect today's tastes and trends.

A problem with trends, however, is that they change quickly and vary depending on where you live. Therefore, before finalizing a new purchase—whether it's paint, flooring, or simply hardware for your cabinets—do a little research to discover the styles and colours that homebuyers in your city are craving.

Visit a variety of show homes to see the products and styles they're using. Builders hire professionals to furnish and decorate their new builds, so these will give you a good indication of what's popular in your city.

Instead of buying the first product you come across at a hardware or big box store, take the time to visit a show room in a specialty store. You don't need to purchase at high-end shops, just drop in to see what the latest trends are so you'll know what to shop for at Canadian Tire or Walmart!

Of course, an ideal way to learn current trends and tastes is to get advice from knowledgeable sales staff or from a professional decorator or home stager.

Kitchens and Bathrooms

Kitchens and bathrooms are consistently reported to be the most important rooms for buyers. Pay particular attention to updating these rooms. You probably don't need to invest in a total kitchen or bathroom remodel, however. Simply focusing on the following upgrades will likely make your house outstanding:

Update Plumbing Fixtures. Updating faucets in the kitchen and bathrooms is a simple way to create a modern and appealing look. In the kitchen, choose a mid-range, attractive faucet that will fit easily into the deck of your sink. Note the number of hole drillings in the deck (one, three, or none), and measure the distance between the centres of each hole. Then choose a faucet that is compatible. (Some new faucets have a base that will cover existing holes.) If necessary, hire a professional to add holes to your sink. Look for a faucet that is both functional and elegant, such as an oversized gooseneck faucet with a pull-down sprayer. If you currently have a side sprayer, consider replacing it with a soap dispenser. Choose a faucet that matches the style and finish of the hardware on the cabinets for a coordinated look.

For the bathroom, choose a faucet that is the right height, depth, and shape for the sink, and make sure its style and finish match the rest of the bathroom. Consider updating the towel bars and toilet paper holder to coordinate with the new faucet. Does the shower head also need updating? If so, choose a style that coordinates with the rest of the room. Dated shower doors can also be replaced with clear, seamless glass.

If you have an older, water-guzzling toilet, consider updating with a new low-flow or dual-flush toilet. If your toilet (and sink) is avocado green or a harvest gold shade from the '70s, it's definitely worth investing in new white fixtures.

If your bathtub is a vintage colour, consider having it professionally re-glazed in bright white. This process (also known as refinishing or re-surfacing) involves bonding a new surface directly over the old tub surface. Another option is to install an acrylic tub surround that adheres directly to the tub walls; as an added bonus, the surround also covers dated or damaged tile. Both options will give you a fresh, updated look without the expense and time required to replace the tub.

Update Counters. Counters make or break the room. Improving kitchen and bathroom counters that are dated or in poor shape makes a dramatic impact. Although many high-end kitchens have quartz, granite or other stone countertops, not all homes need them. Make sure your house measures up to the standards of your neighbourhood and price range.

If your competitors have granite counters, consider adding them to your house. However, granite is very expensive and not easily changed. If the layout of your kitchen is less than ideal, then granite counters may be a deterrent because they would make future renovations even more costly and difficult. Therefore, if you need to replace your countertop but granite would require other major renovations or is not necessarily expected in a house in your price range, then consider other options:

- **Replace with new laminate countertops.** Laminate is reasonably affordable and can look terrific. Choose a neutral colour that complements the colour of the cabinets; avoid bold patterns. Instead of including a laminate backsplash piece, add a tile backsplash for a stylish feature.

- **Install a solid surface counter.** Solid surface counters are a mixture of manmade materials. Corian brand is an example. They come in a range of colours, patterns, and finishes and can look very similar to stone. Unlike laminate and tile, a solid surface counter is seamless, stain resistant, and easily repaired if it's dented, chipped, or scratched. This option is more pricey than laminate, but more affordable than granite.

- **Add granite overlay on top of your existing counters.** You can hire a company to permanently bond a thin slab of granite or other stone onto your existing counters. The result looks great and has all the benefits of a slab of granite but is a fraction of the cost and requires no demolition. Installation is quick and usually can be done in a day.

- **Install granite on the kitchen island only.** If you have an island, consider upgrading its top to a stone finish. Because the island is the focal point of the kitchen, adding granite here will be dramatic enough that you can leave the rest of the counters in laminate (make sure the colours complement each other). If the island top is very small, ask about granite off cuts, which are sold at a reduced rate.

Update Cabinets. Like countertops, cabinets are a major feature that can make or break the kitchen or bathroom. If your cabinets are old or dated but otherwise in good shape, consider either painting or re-facing them for a more contemporary look. Some people are reluctant to paint over "good wood." Regardless of the quality, if it's outdated, you're far better to update it with a current paint colour than to leave it in its original condition. Re-facing involves replacing the door and drawer fronts rather than the entire cabinet. Painting and re-facing are both economical alternatives to a full kitchen renovation. When choosing new cabinet fronts or colour, look for warm wood tones or light, fresh finishes. Also, simple Shaker-style cabinets are currently the most popular style and are better for resale. Check out cabinet colors and styles in local show homes are to get a good idea of what's on-trend in your area.

Update Hardware. Who would expect that changing cabinet knobs, pulls, and handles could make such a dramatic improvement? Outdated, tarnished, or damaged hardware makes the entire kitchen or bathroom dated and drab. Replacing them will instantly perk up the entire room. Choose hardware that suits the style and finish of your faucets and fits in well with the style of the cabinets and room. Avoid hardware in cutesy shapes or funky colours. Choose a neutral, elegant style. You don't have to stop at the kitchen and bathrooms. You can update hardware on cabinets, doors, and drawers throughout the house, but if you must prioritize, update just the kitchen and then bathrooms. For a coordinated look, use similar hardware throughout the house. Check at a cabinet retailer or your local home centre for a good selection of knobs and handles. For online shopping, try ordering through Homedepot.ca, Ikea.com, or Jackandjade.ca.

Best Upgrades Throughout the House

Although upgraded kitchens and bathrooms are very important to home-buyers, so is the overall appearance and maintenance of the rest of the living space. Upgrades that generate the greatest return on investment include applying new paint, installing new light fixtures, and upgrading the flooring.

Paint

The power of paint is amazing. Painting is one of the most important upgrades you can make when staging your home. Reasonably inexpensive, easy to do, and with quick results, painting a room gives an excellent return for your efforts. Fresh paint in the right colour not only improves the look of a room, it can also influence its "mood," transforming a room into a dramatic and energizing experience or giving it a calm, inviting "stay a while" atmosphere.

Years ago, a typical seller wouldn't paint the house before selling, thinking that new owners would want to choose their own colour. This approach doesn't work anymore, as we've seen houses languish on the market until they get that fresh coat of neutral paint. Perhaps this is because homebuyers want to see the house at its best rather than imagine its potential. Or perhaps it's because neutral colours buy time for the new owners; even if they want to eventually change the colour, they can live comfortably with a neutral colour until they are ready to make their own changes. Whatever the reason, it is safest to give buyers what they want by painting the rooms for them.

If your walls have scuffmarks and chipped paint, a fresh coat of paint is in order. Even if your walls are in good condition, we recommend painting if their current colour is bold or unusual. Painting walls a neutral colour makes them appealing to the greatest number of buyers.

Dated honey-coloured oak cabinets in this room were painted a neutral cream to update the look and blend in nicely with the walls.

Many homes designed in the 1980s have oak accents throughout, such as oak cabinets, trim, bannisters, and railings. Painting over oak with a clean white or cream colour makes the house look more modern. However, painting trim can be tricky because unless it's a bedroom or bathroom with a clear cut-off, you'll have to paint the trim throughout the entire house. If you are going to repaint the whole house, then consider painting over the oak trim as well. Otherwise, consider just painting some of the other oak accents, such as cabinets, railings, and bannisters.

The Trouble with Wallpaper

While you're looking at your walls and deciding whether to paint, check out your wallpaper. Don't have any? Good. If you do have wallpaper, get stripping (the wallpaper, that is).

Most people don't want wallpaper when they move in. Even if they like wallpaper in general, it's a risk to assume they'll like your choice. Wallpaper is very taste-specific. Very few people will like the same pattern, and what's pleasing to one person may not be to another. Wallpaper borders around the room and completely papered walls are major buyer deterrents because removing them requires significant time and effort. Buyers may choose to walk away rather than deal with the wallpaper.

If you need to remove wallpaper, consider renting a wallpaper steamer. This handy electrical device applies steam over the wallpaper, loosening the adhesive and making the paper easier to remove. Be careful using a steamer on drywall, however, because drywall is vulnerable to moisture and could get damaged by the steam.

Choosing Interior Paint Colours. The right wall colour is crucial for a well-staged room; you need a colour that is fresh, on-trend, and appealing to most people. For staging purposes, Brandy O'Brien and Joline Throssell, co-owners of Blended Jive Paint and Décor, recommend choosing a classic light- to medium-toned neutral colour that complements your furnishings and flooring. "These colours will open up the space and give a clean crisp look, making the room a welcoming environment," says O'Brien. Best of all, they will be easy for new buyers to live with.

Neutrals don't have to be boring. Each year, paint manufacturers introduce new variations of "designer's choice" neutrals. To see the current neutral colours, visit paint manufacturers' websites (such as benjamin-moore.com or para.com). Also consult a professional home stager or the colour specialist at a paint store for advice on what colours to choose and where to apply them.

Whatever brand you decide to use, it's always worth the extra money to use high-quality paints because they are easier to apply, require fewer coats, and are more durable than lower quality paints.

The following are some tips to keep in mind when choosing paint colour:

- Use no more than three tones of the same colour throughout the house to give a nice flow between rooms and create a spacious feel. Some clients feel that this is not enough colour, but when selling your home, adding colour with accessories is far better than adding colours to the walls. As you'll see in Chapter 6, colourful accessories placed in the right way add personality and punch to a room.

- When applying your colour, follow the 60:30:10 rule. Cover 60 percent of the walls with one tone, 30 percent with another tone, and 10 percent with the darkest tone. The darkest tone serves as an accent colour, giving extra prominence to special areas (e.g., a feature wall or the wall surrounding a fireplace). The light and medium tones can be used interchangeably throughout the rest of the house.

- Darker colours give the illusion of the wall advancing, and lighter colours seem to make the wall recede. Therefore, use the medium-toned colour in large rooms to make them feel cozier and more intimate, and use the lighter-toned colour in small rooms to make them feel more open and spacious.

- Colours can be considered cool or warm. Cool colours are based on blues, magentas, and greens. They tend to make rooms look more spacious and work well in south- or west-facing rooms with a lot of light and sun. Warm colours are based on reds, browns, oranges, and yellows. They work well in north- or east-facing rooms that have a cooler light because they make the room feel cozier and warmer.

- Before deciding on a colour, bring home large paint chips or a sample pot of colour and test them in different light conditions. Observe them at different times of the day and evening. Also carefully evaluate how the colour looks with your furniture and flooring.

- Ideally, paint all areas that can be seen from the main floor, including the front hallway, kitchen, dining room, living room, adjoining hallways, stairways, and even the upstairs landing if it's visible from the main floor. Paint all walls (except perhaps those in the bathrooms and bedrooms) in one of the three shades of your chosen colour. Because the bathrooms and bedrooms are separate from the main living areas, you may choose a different neutral paint colour for these rooms.

- Paint over any stains on the ceiling. Hire a professional, if necessary, to ensure the fresh paint blends in with the rest of the ceiling. Only repaint the entire ceiling if absolutely necessary; unless it's a bedroom or bathroom, you'll have to continue painting the ceiling throughout the house. If you decide to repaint the ceiling, consider painting it a lighter shade of the wall colour (¼ strength works well). This will create a blended feel with the walls rather than a sharp contrast.

- If you have the time and budget, consider repainting interior doors and trim to freshen the look. Trim includes baseboards, window frames, and doorframes. Painting the doors and all the trim throughout the house the same colour creates continuity and flow between the rooms. We usually recommend a warm white, such as "Cloud White" from Benjamin Moore. For a blended look, paint the doors and baseboards a paler shade of the walls.

Choosing a "Green" Paint

Conventional paints contain high levels of VOCs (volatile organic compounds), which are chemicals that are released into the air when the paint is applied and may continue being released for years (known as off-gassing).

Evidence suggests that exposure to certain mixtures of VOCs can cause serious health problems. According to the Environmental Protection Agency, concentrations of VOCs are up to 10 times higher indoors than outdoors. Many home products other than paints contain VOCs, such as cleansers and disinfectants, air fresheners, solvents, and glues. It is always wise to reduce your exposure to VOCs as much as possible.

Homeowners are becoming increasingly aware of the side effects of chemicals and possible health issues. As a result, most paint manufacturers now offer low-VOC and zero-VOC products. Although these paints are more expensive, they generally apply well, produce fewer odors, dry quicker, and are less harmful to people and the environment.

Choosing the Right Finish. After choosing the colour, the next step is selecting the finish. Different finishes have varying levels of sheen (i.e., shine) and different applications:

- **Matte, or flat,** is a very smooth, dull finish with almost no shine. It tends to collect dirt and can't be scrubbed hard. This is generally used on ceilings.

- **Flat Enamel** also has a low sheen but is more durable than a matte finish. It is best for walls with uneven finishes (to hide imperfections) or walls in older homes.

- **Eggshell** is another low-shine finish. It has the smooth look of a flat paint, but has a touch of shine that enables it to be cleaned easily. Eggshell finishes are appropriate for all interior walls that don't require frequent cleaning, such as bedrooms, offices, dining rooms, and living rooms.

- **Satin, or pearl,** is a slightly shinier finish than eggshell, but is more durable for more frequent cleaning and light scrubbing. It is often used for window and door trim and baseboards and on walls in bathrooms, kitchens, hallways—anywhere that requires frequent cleaning or light scrubbing.

- **Glossy** is the shiniest of all the finishes. It is rarely used on interior walls but sometimes on kitchen cabinets for a contemporary look. Because of the very high sheen, imperfections will be greatly magnified so excellent preparation is required.

Lighting

Installing new light fixtures is another easy upgrade that yields a good return on investment and dramatically improves the look of a home. Old light fixtures and lamps (and even old light switches and outlet cover plates) quickly make a home look dated. If your light fixtures are more than 8 to 10 years old, seriously consider replacing them.

Ideally, replace all fixtures in the house with a similar style and finish so there's continuity between rooms. However, if that's not practical, update the fixtures in the most important rooms: the entryway, dining room, bathrooms, and master bedroom. Updating lamps in your living room may also be worth the effort.

You don't have to spend a lot. Hardware and home improvement stores have good quality, modern light fixtures for $100 to $150. It's always helpful to consult with a knowledgeable salesperson at a lighting store for advice.

If you prefer to shop online, we recommend Unionlightingandfurnishings.com and Clicklightingandhome.com. Both are Canadian sites and ship anywhere in Canada. Potterybarn.com also has a good lighting selection, and they now ship to Canada.

The following are some guidelines to consider when choosing new fixtures:

- Choose fixtures with some decorative detail if your home is furnished in a more traditional style. Look for sleeker, simpler fixtures if your home is more contemporary.

- Choose a fixture that's in scale with the size of the room. Many people tend to choose light fixtures that are too small for the space. Err on the side of larger, not smaller, fixtures.

- In long hallways, place a fixture approximately every 8 to 10 feet. Whether you install a flush-mount or semi-flush fixture or a chandelier will depend on your hallway ceiling height. Whichever type of fixture you choose, install it so its bottom is at least 7 feet above the floor.

- Chandeliers have become popular in bedrooms and even in bathrooms and kitchens. A beautiful fixture over your bed will add luxurious sparkle to the bedroom. Look for a small chandelier to hang in your ensuite. In the kitchen, a simple chandelier over the sink adds sophistication.

- To determine the ideal width for a chandelier, measure the width of the room (in feet) and double it. The width of the fixture is this number in inches. For example: an 11-foot-wide room would require a 22-inch-wide fixture (11 feet x 2 = 22 feet; therefore width of fixture is 22 inches).

- To determine the ideal height for a chandelier, measure the height of the room and allow 2½ to 3 inches for each foot. For example, if your room has a 9-foot high ceiling, try to get a chandelier that is about 22½ to 27 inches tall.

- In a dining room, choose a fixture that is half as wide as the width of the tabletop. For example, if the dining room table is 48 inches wide, a chandelier that is about 24 inches across would look ideal. Hang the chandelier over the centre of the table. In a dining

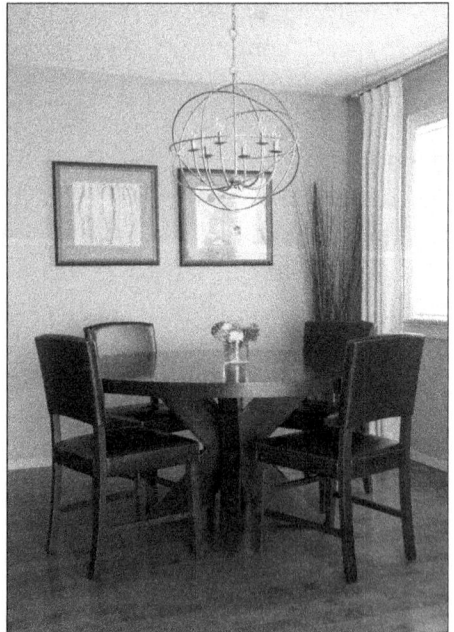

The bottom of this chandelier hangs 30 inches above the tabletop.

room with eight-foot ceilings, hang a chandelier about 30 to 32 inches above the tabletop. With nine-foot ceilings, hang the chandelier about 33 to 35 inches above the tabletop. For ceilings nine feet high or more, choose a two-tiered chandelier to help fill the space.

- If you're hanging a chandelier in an entryway, centre it in the room and make sure its bottom is at least 7 feet above the floor. If there are windows in this area, hang the fixture so it is centred in the window and can be seen from outside.

- When hanging pendant lighting over a kitchen island, set the bottom of the fixture about 30 inches above the work surface.

- Having one central overhead fixture in a living room is outdated. Add sconces and lamps to bounce light off the ceilings and walls, visually expanding the size of the room.

- In living rooms, hang wall sconces about 5 feet from the floor and 6 to 8 feet apart.

Flooring

Although replacing flooring is another upgrade with a good return on investment (50 to 75%), think carefully before doing it. If your carpets are in passable, though not perfect, condition, all they may need is a good steam cleaning. You can then stage the house to direct buyers' attention away from the floor and onto more appealing features.

If your carpeting, tile, or vinyl flooring is in very poor condition or has a bold colour or pattern, it will drop the value of your house. If you decide to upgrade your flooring, consider the following tips:

- Choose flooring options that are in line with the price range of your house. If houses that you are competing with have hardwood floors and ceramic tile, then consider installing them as well. If laminate and vinyl flooring are standard in your price range, then go with those options.

- Choose larger tiles over smaller tiles to help the room feel more spacious. For example, choose 12-inch tiles instead of 8-inch tiles.

- Choose flooring that fits in well with the style of the house. For example, in older heritage homes, hardwood flooring is more suitable than wall-to-wall carpeting.

- Limit the number of flooring changes in a smaller space. Too many variations in the flooring (such as carpet in one room, tile in the foyer beside it, and vinyl in the next room) make the space seem small and chopped up.

- You don't have to install top-of-the line material, but don't cut corners. Skip the bargain bin options and don't choose laminate if other houses in your price range have hardwood. It's best to go with a mid-priced flooring option.

- Choose a neutral-coloured flooring that complements the rest of the room.

- Install a thick under pad to make carpeting feel luxurious.

- For area rugs, choose neutral-coloured, non-patterned rugs that are a shade lighter or darker than the flooring.

Repairs and Upgrades CHECKLIST

The following are some of the most common repairs and upgrades required throughout the house. Before purchasing upgrades, find out what colours and styles are most popular with homebuyers in your area.

Ceilings

Repairs:

☐ Paint over water stains on the ceilings (after repairing the problem that caused the stain). Alternatively, mix equal parts bleach and water in a spray bottle and lightly spray over the stain, being careful not to over saturate. Let dry and the stain should disappear.

☐ Ensure ceiling fans are in good repair. Fix any squeaks.

Upgrades:

☐ Repaint the ceiling, if necessary.

Walls

Repairs:

☐ Repair any holes or large dents with spackling compound and paint.

☐ Repair rotting wood, large cracks, and flaking paint.

Upgrades:

☐ Remove wallpaper and borders.

☐ Apply fresh paint if the walls are in poor condition or their current colour is bold or dated; choose a neutral colour in an eggshell finish.

☐ Repaint the trim if necessary.

Stairs

Repairs:

☐ Repair loose or broken stair handrails.

☐ Repair or replace tread surfaces.

☐ Ensure carpeting is secure on stairs.

Upgrades:

❑ Paint or upgrade the railing system if necessary (follow building codes).

Windows

Repairs:

❑ Ensure windows open easily and close tightly.

❑ Ensure window locks and hardware are in good working condition.

❑ Repair or replace weather stripping or caulking if needed (caulking usually needs replacing after 6 to 7 years).

❑ Check for condensation on the windows, a sign of excessive moisture levels. A dehumidifier may eliminate the problem.

❑ Repair or replace screens. Consider removing and storing screens to let in more light. In winter, removing screens may reduce condensation.

Upgrades:

❑ Replace windows if needed (e.g., replace all broken or cracked windows and windows with fogging between the panes of glass, indicating a broken seal).

❑ Replace rotting window frames.

Doors

Repairs:

❑ Ensure all doors, including bifolds, open easily and close tightly.

❑ Oil squeaky hinges and tighten screws.

❑ Replace worn weather stripping.

❑ Ensure doorknobs and locks are in good repair.

❑ Ensure cabinet doors open and close smoothly and are level.

❑ Repair loose hinges on cabinets.

Upgrades:

❑ Paint doors as needed. Choose a good quality, semi-gloss paint. Paint the door the same colour as the frame and baseboards.

❑ Replace doors as needed.

- ❑ Paint, reface, or replace cabinets if they are in poor condition or are a dated or non-neutral colour.
- ❑ Update doorknobs and pulls on cabinets and drawers.

Floors

Repairs:

- ❑ Repair squeaky floorboards.
- ❑ Repair scratches on hardwood. For a small scratch, apply a stain marker in a matching colour along the scratch. For deeper scratches, apply a wax made for floor scratches and then the marker. Choose a wax colour that closely matches your floor. These are not permanent fixes, but will make the scratches less noticeable.
- ❑ Strip and reseal hardwood floors if they are in poor shape.
- ❑ Repair damaged ceramic tile.
- ❑ Repair chipped, disintegrating, or stained grouting.
- ❑ Glue down any curling edges of vinyl flooring.
- ❑ Tack down any loose or curling edges on carpets.

Upgrades:

- ❑ Replace badly stained, damaged, worn, or bold-coloured flooring.

Lights/Electrical

Repairs:

- ❑ Replace burned out bulbs with the highest wattage bulb recommended for the fixture.
- ❑ Ensure all light switches and smoke detectors function properly.
- ❑ Ensure range hood and bathroom fans are operating properly.

Upgrades:

- ❑ Replace outdated lamps and light fixtures, especially in front entrance, dining room, bathrooms, master bedroom, and living room.
- ❑ Update light switch and outlet covers.
- ❑ Install dimmer switches in the dining room and living rooms.

Plumbing

Repairs:

- ☐ Repair dripping faucets.

- ☐ Unclog slow drains.

- ☐ Replace any old, dried, or stained caulking around sinks, backsplashes, tubs, and shower.

Upgrades:

- ☐ Update faucets.

- ☐ Replace toilet if it has a dated colour; install a white 6-litre or dual-flush toilet.

- ☐ Re-glaze tub if it is a dated colour or install an acrylic tub surround.

Countertops

Repairs:

- ☐ Replace chipped, moldy, or disintegrating grout around tiles.

- ☐ Replace old, dried, or stained caulking.

- ☐ Glue and clamp any loose edging on laminate countertops.

Upgrades:

- ☐ Paint or replace the countertop if it is in poor condition or is a non-neutral colour.

chapter five

Step 3: Cleaning

THE THIRD STEP TO STAGING your home is cleaning it. Let's face it, no one wants to see someone else's dirt and grime, much less consider moving into it. Most people feel stressed and uncomfortable in a dirty room, but a clean room is a stress reliever.

Cleaning your home is the surest way to earn maximum dollars with minimal investment. A recent HomeGain survey estimated that the average cost of cleaning a house is $200, and the expected home price increase is $1700. That's a 750% return on your investment!

Of course everyone knows they should clean their house before selling it, but you'd be surprised by how many sellers don't do it well enough. Cleaning a house to stage it is not the same as cleaning it for a guest. Unlike guests, potential buyers will look in cupboards, open drawers, check out your bedroom, and inspect the inside of your oven. Rather than your usual surface cleaning, you will need to do a detailed deep cleaning. Anywhere a potential buyer is likely to look is a place that needs to be cleaned.

Sound a little obsessive? It is, but that's the look to strive for. A sparkling clean house sends the message that you are a perfectionist. And perfectionists are careful and attentive homeowners: as soon as a problem arises, they take care of it. Potential buyers will assume that if you were particular enough to clean the baseboards, surely you also promptly attended to leaky roofs and cleaned your furnace filters every month.

Make sure to give yourself plenty of time to get everything done, especially in the kitchen and bathrooms. If you don't have the time, energy, or inclination to do it yourself, hire a cleaning service to do it for you or help with some of the job. Money invested in cleaning will be money well spent.

Once you've completed the deep cleaning, keeping the house clean and preparing it for last minute showings will be a snap. And because you've already de-cluttered your house, the most difficult part of cleaning is already done. So channel your inner June Cleaver, roll up the sleeves of your vintage '50s cardigan, and prepare to clean it like you mean it.

Getting Started

Before you start, make sure you have everything you need in a tote or bucket that you can carry from room to room. Here are the basic cleaning products to have on hand:

- All-purpose cleaner
- Glass cleaner
- Bathroom cleaner
- Oven cleaner
- Toilet bowl cleaner

If you're trying a new cleaning product, it's important to always test it in an inconspicuous area first to make sure it won't damage the surface. Follow all instructions on the labels, being careful to use the product that is right for each surface. Of course, never mix different cleaners; they could react violently or cause toxic fumes.

In addition to the above cleaning products, have the following supplies handy:

- **Microfiber cloths**. The tiny fibers in these lint-free cloths pick up dirt, dust, bacteria, and grease better than ordinary rags. They require less cleaning product and, depending on the quality of the cloth, clean effectively with only water. They can be tossed in the washing machine, air dried, and then reused.
- **Static duster**. A static duster grabs and holds onto dust, dirt, and cobwebs. If possible, get a duster on an extendable pole to reach high ceilings and bookshelves.

- **Mop**. For hardwood floors, use a flat-head mop with a detachable cotton or microfibre cloth.

- **Squeegee**. A small squeegee is useful for cleaning windows and removing excess water in showers and tubs.

Choosing "Green" Cleaners

Because you will be doing a lot of cleaning, you may want to consider using "green" cleaning options to limit your exposure to dangerous chemicals and to be kind to the environment. When buying green cleaning products, look for the following descriptions on the label: phosphate-free, chlorine-free, non-toxic, and biodegradable. Green cleaners also state on their labels that they are either unscented or scented with natural plant-derived scents or essential oils. Check for ingredients like alcohol, coconut or other plant oils, or plant oil disinfectants such as rosemary.

Many people make their own cleaners from simple household ingredients like baking soda, vinegar, borax, and lemon juice. Homemade cleaners are natural, biodegradable, non-toxic, and a fraction of the price of commercial cleaners. You can find many recipes online for natural cleaners. However, if you choose to use homemade cleaners, keep in mind that they usually require extra elbow grease and a lot more rinsing than you might expect. They can also damage the surface if you're not careful. Vinegar, especially, is very acidic and can damage grout, caulk, and granite. Always research how and where to use a homemade cleaner, and always test the cleaner in an inconspicuous area first.

- **Mr. Clean Magic Eraser**. This product has many uses and is very effective for gently cleaning surfaces that would otherwise require a lot of scrubbing. It's especially good for removing marks (including scuff marks, adhesive residue, and crayon) on walls and baseboards, removing soap scum in tubs and showers, and cleaning tile and grout. Always test on an inconspicuous area first, though, to make sure it doesn't damage the finish.

- **Toothbrush**. Get a few toothbrushes with firm nylon bristles to clean in crevices and tight corners, such as the grimy area around bathroom faucets and the grooves around recessed door panels.
- **Scrub brush**. Have a stiff-bristled brush handy for jobs needing intense scrubbing, such as cleaning stained grout.

Cleaning Tips and Tasks

The following section describes general cleaning tips; it also details cleaning tasks for every room and extra cleaning considerations for specific rooms and areas. The checklist at the end of the chapter summarizes these cleaning tasks.

If you're short on time, focus on cleaning the kitchen and bathrooms first because dirt in these rooms is easily noticed and is a major buyer deterrent. Having clean windows is also a high priority, especially in the main living areas and the front entryway, because clean windows help to brighten the room.

You can simplify the cleaning process if you make sure the room is tidy before you begin cleaning. For example, before cleaning the kitchen, do the dishes and deal with any papers or mail that may have accumulated since you last de-cluttered.

Clean from top to bottom so that dust and dirt will fall down and not settle on cleaned areas. For example, when cleaning walls, start at the ceiling and clean down to the baseboards and floor; when vacuuming the stairs, begin at the top and work down to the bottom. Also clean from left to right so that you know what you've done.

Cleaning Tips and Tasks for Every Room

When deep cleaning the house, you will repeat certain tasks in each room. The following are general cleaning tasks for each room:

Ceilings:

- Use an extendable duster to remove dust strings or cobwebs from ceilings and in the corners of the walls.
- Clean all ceiling-mounted light fixtures and ceiling fans. **To clean a light fixture**, remove the fixture and wash it in the sink with warm

water and a little dishwashing liquid. If the fixture is covered in kitchen grease, add a little household ammonia to the water. Rinse well and dry before replacing. **To clean a ceiling fan**, stand on a ladder to comfortably reach the fan. Dust around the base, fan arms, and the tops and bottoms of the fan blades. Wipe the blades with a cloth sprayed with all-purpose cleaner. If the fan has a light fixture, remove the fixture and wash in warm, soapy water. Rinse and dry before replacing.

Walls:

- Working from the top to the bottom, dust the wall first, and then spot clean with a damp microfibre cloth and mild detergent (optional). Gently rub stains or scuffs with a Magic Eraser or a baking soda and water paste (3 parts baking soda to 1 part water). Use a degreaser product if necessary. Always test products in an inconspicuous area, such as inside a closet, before using on a visible part of the wall.

- As you work down the walls, use a damp cloth and mild detergent to clean light switches and switch plates. If the grooves in the switches are grimy, clean them with a cotton swab or toothbrush dipped in cleaner.

- Dust and wash the baseboards with an all-purpose cleaner. A toothbrush might be useful to reach into corners.

- Dust and clean all wall décor, including mirrors and picture frames. Use a soft, lint-free cloth and glass cleaner to clean glass. To protect the art, dampen the cloth with cleaner rather than spraying directly onto the picture frames.

Windows:

- Clean screens, windows, tracks, and windowsills. Remove screens, and vacuum them or hose them down outside. If the screens are not needed, leave them out to let in as much natural light as possible and to highlight the view. Spray glass cleaner onto the window, and then wipe with a clean microfibre cloth, paper towel, or squeegee. Polish the glass with a clean cloth. Wash the exterior of the window as well. (Consider hiring a professional to clean hard-to-reach windows.) If you wipe the interior of the window vertically and the exterior horizontally (or vice versa), then if there are any streaks, you'll be able to tell which side they're on. Spray the cleaner into the window tracks and wipe down with a cloth or toothbrush. Dust and wash windowsills with warm, soapy water.

- Clean all window treatments (blinds and draperies). Vacuum drapes and wash according to the manufacturer's instructions. Machine wash sheer curtains in the delicate cycle; hang to dry. Clean blinds by closing the slats and then wiping each with a slightly damp cloth. Then open and close the slats in the opposite direction and wipe each slat again. If you have plastic mini-blinds that are quite dirty, put them in the bath filled with warm water and about a cup of vinegar (or dishwashing liquid or even Pine Sol) and let them soak for about half and hour. Wipe them down in the tub, and let them air dry on a towel on the floor.

Doors:

- Clean doors and door frames. Remove all stickers, nameplates, or hooks from the door. Use a degreaser or Magic Eraser to remove scuffs and stains. Clean the front, back, and sides of the door, including the doorknobs. Remember to clean the top of the frame and work down the sides. For patio doors, clean between the tracks, and wash the glass doors with glass cleaner and a clean cloth.

All surfaces:

- Dust every surface in the room. Use a clean, damp microfibre cloth to dust most objects, including wood furniture, shelves, accessories, and so on. Make sure the cloth isn't too wet or it could damage some surfaces or leave streaks. Dampen it just enough to pick up dust without leaving moisture behind. Rinse the cloth often or use a fresh cloth as needed. Use a dry cloth to polish if necessary.

- Be careful when cleaning wood surfaces. Choose a product (whether oil, wax, or polish) appropriate for the finish.

- Lift and dust each object and then dust underneath it. Remember to also dust your books and electronics.

- Use a vacuum cleaner attachment or a static duster to clean lampshades. Wipe down the lamp base, and dust the bulb after allowing it to cool.

Floors:

- Vacuum or sweep floors. Sprinkle baking soda over the carpets before vacuuming to remove odors. Move furniture to clean underneath. Make sure to clean all the corners.

- Using a mop and floor cleaner (or all purpose cleaner diluted with hot water), mop the floor. If you have hardwood, check with the manufacturer's recommendations for which cleaning product to use. Some recommend only using a mop or cloth slightly dampened with plain water. Mop in small sections at a time, beginning at the farthest corner from the door and moving towards the door. Remove scuffmarks on vinyl flooring by sprinkling baking soda over the mark and wiping with a damp cloth.

- Steam clean carpets and upholstery. Consider hiring a professional if your carpet or upholstery is stained; otherwise, you can rent a steam cleaner and do it yourself.

Cleaning Tips and Tasks For Specific Rooms

Assuming that you have already thoroughly de-cluttered each room and wiped down the insides of cabinets as you de-cluttered (see Chapter 3), you can now finish cleaning the rooms. The following are tasks for each room that are in addition to the above tasks:

Kitchen:

- Clean the stove: For electric stoves, remove burner rings and drip pans and let them soak in warm, soapy water. For gas stoves, remove and soak the grates. Wipe down the top of the stove using hot, soapy water and a clean cloth. Clean the range hood and control panel, removing fingerprints and greasy residue (you may need to use a degreaser). Finish off the stovetop by polishing smooth surfaces with a glass cleaner. Next, pull out the oven and clean its sides and front. Vacuum under the oven. Wash and dry the burner rings, drip pans, or grates that have been soaking. If the burner rings and drip pans still don't look great, buy new replacements. Clean the inside of the oven according to manufacturer's instructions, and remember to clean the inside of the oven door.

- Clean inside and outside your fridge using a soft cloth and warm, soapy water. While you're at it, wipe down the dusty grate under the door. Pull the fridge out and vacuum its back and underneath it. Remove items from one shelf or drawer at a time and thoroughly clean the shelf or drawer. When you're done, place an open box of baking soda on a shelf to absorb odors.

- Wash the exterior of the dishwasher and inside of the door. Also clean any splatters on the cabinets beside the dishwasher.

- Clean inside the microwave with a damp cloth. If there are baked-on stains, first place a cup of water in the centre of microwave and turn the power on high for three minutes. The steam will help loosen the grime. Remove the glass plate and wash it in soapy water. Clean outside the microwave with a cloth sprayed with all-purpose cleaner. Finally, clean the counter under the microwave.

- Wash the table and chairs, including the legs.

- Wash the cabinet doors. You might only need to use a microfibre cloth dampened with plain water. If you need more cleaning power, fill the sink with warm water and add a little degreaser or liquid dish soap. Rinse the cloth often. Clean the undersides of hanging cabinets, where grease and food splashes accumulate. Clean all knobs and hardware as well.

- Clean all grout and tile in the kitchen. Dampen the grout and apply baking soda, then scrub clean with a toothbrush or scrub brush.

- Wash countertops. Instead of using abrasive cleansers on countertops, remove stains with a baking soda and water paste. If you've left an appliance on the countertop for display, wash and polish it.

- Clean garbage cans, inside and out. Sprinkle about half a cup of baking soda into the bottom of the can to absorb odors. The baking soda will last for two to three months.

- Wash the sink. Use a toothbrush to scrub away dirt in the edges of the drain, faucet, and taps. Use a nonabrasive bathroom cleaner to clean stainless steel, enamel, or porcelain sinks. Remove stains by sprinkling baking soda over them and then rubbing clean. Finish the job by polishing with a glass cleaner. Dry and buff until the sink and taps sparkle.

Cleaning Stainless Steel

Stainless steel is popular in kitchens, but it can easily scratch if you use the wrong cleaner on it. The simplest way to clean stainless steel is with a microfibre cloth dampened with plain water. Wipe in the direction of the grain, and then dry to remove streaks.

For more cleaning power, use a cloth dipped into a mixture of warm water and mild dishwashing liquid. Rinse and dry thoroughly.

Use a glass cleaner or commercial stainless steel cleaner to remove fingerprints and to polish the steel (test first in an inconspicuous area). Alternatively, apply a thin coating of extra virgin olive oil onto the surface, and then polish with a clean cloth.

Bathrooms:

- Dust or vacuum the exhaust fan.

- Clean the tub and surrounding area. If the tile or tub surround extends to the ceiling, use a flat-head mop to reach the top. Clean all grout and tile surfaces using a scrub brush or toothbrush. Use a toothbrush to clean around the taps and drain and other hard-to-reach areas. Remember to clean the soap dish, showerhead, tub ledge, and corners of the tub. Rinse thoroughly, and then dry and shine the tub and chrome surfaces with a clean cloth. (A product called Gel-Gloss gives tubs and surrounds a protective and lustrous shine.) To clean a glass shower door, apply bathroom cleaner to it and let it sit for a few minutes; then clean with a scrub brush. Also clean the door runners and tracks with a toothbrush if necessary. Finish by polishing the door with a glass cleaner.

- Wash the shower curtain in the washing machine; if it has a busy pattern or bold colour—or if it's plastic—consider replacing it with a solid cream or white fabric shower curtain and liner. If the shower curtain bar is rusty replace it as well, and also replace plastic curtain rings with shiny new metal rings.

- Clean the vanity. Make sure small appliances and toiletries are neatly stored out of sight. When washing the countertop, also clean the backsplash, the wall around the sink, the drawers, and the cabinets (including hardware). If necessary, use a toothbrush to clean all the grooves and crevices around the taps and drain. Use glass cleaner to clean the taps and faucet. Remember to also clean the soap dish or pump dispenser.
- Clean the toilet, inside and out. Also wipe under the tank, dust the water supply line, and wash around the seat hinges and floor bolts.

Bedrooms:

- Vacuum or dust the headboard and footboard.
- Strip the bed and launder the bedspread or duvet cover and pillowcases.
- If possible, hang duvets, pillows, and quilts outside in the sun for a few hours. The fresh air and sunlight will sanitize them and freshen up the room.
- Open the window to air out the room.
- Vacuum or sweep the floor, including inside the closet and behind the door.

Living Room, Family Room, Dining Room:

- Clean built-in wall units, bookshelves, or other large furniture from top to bottom. Lift and dust each item on the shelf, and then dust underneath the item.
- Dust plants by wiping them gently with a damp cloth.
- Dust and clean the dining table, chairs, and coffee tables. Use a slightly damp microfibre cloth.
- Remove cushions and throw pillows from couches and chairs, and vacuum the cushions and upholstery. Vacuum underneath the furniture. Steam clean the upholstery or hire a professional cleaning service to do it.
- Clean your leather furniture. Use a commercial cleaner recommended by the manufacturer, or carefully wipe with a slightly damp cloth.

Apply a leather conditioner to restore moisture and sheen.

- Clean the fireplace. Remove the soot, and then scrub the surfaces with water and all-purpose cleaner. Rinse well.

Laundry Room:

- Wipe down the washer and dryer with a damp cloth.
- Pull out the washer and dryer and vacuum behind and underneath them.
- Clean the tops of counters or worktables with a damp cloth.
- Shake out scatter rugs or mats. Vacuum and wash the mats, or replace them with new mats.
- Clean laundry bags and hampers.

Basement/Garage:

- If the basement is finished, deep clean as you would for the living room/family room.
- If the basement is unfinished, sweep the floor and wipe down the furnace and water heater. Make sure all items in the basement are neatly organized.
- Clean or replace the furnace filter.
- If you notice a musty odor in the basement, use a dehumidifier to reduce humidity to a comfortable level (often between 30% and 60%, depending on the season and what part of the country you live in).
- Make sure the floor drain contains water; refill if necessary to prevent smells.
- In the garage, make sure all items are neatly arranged. Sweep the floor.

Eliminating and Preventing Odors

Every house has a unique smell, and this smell is one of the first things to greet potential buyers as they enter.

Smells may originate from fresh baking, flowers, cooking spice, perfume, cleaning detergent, or soap. Unfortunately, not all smells are as innocuous. Common sources of unpleasant odors include dust, dirt, mold, mildew, cigarette smoke, and pets. Usually homeowners have become so accustomed to the odors in their house they don't even notice them.

Smells in your home can kill the sale before buyers even look at the house's features. Even if the house has great curb appeal and a welcoming front entrance, if it has a strong odor, most buyers will immediately be turned off. It's very important to ask someone who doesn't live in the house to tell you if there are any smells you need to eliminate before putting the house on the market.

Many people use heavily scented air fresheners, plug-ins, or candles to hide odors. However, we don't recommend using scented products. Products like these have very strong smells, and buyers will wonder what you're trying to cover up. Often buyers can smell the offending odor *and* the room freshener, which is not a pleasant combination. Also, many people have allergies or sensitivities to these products, so they may not even be able to view your home without getting sick. It's always better to deal with the cause of the odor rather than trying to cover it up.

Fortunately, de-cluttering and thoroughly cleaning your house will help to eliminate many odors, especially those associated with dust and dirt. It's especially important to clean all bedding, drapes, and upholstery, which harbor odors.

After you finish deep cleaning your house, ask a friend for an honest opinion on whether there are any lingering odors. The first step to eliminating odors is figuring out where they are coming from. Is the smell from old sneakers? Rotting food? A musty basement? You'll have to do a sniff test throughout the house to locate the smells.

Once you find the source of the smell, remove it (if possible) and clean the area with a neutralizing cleanser or with a vinegar and water solution. Open the doors and windows to let in fresh air. Follow up by leaving ½ cup of vinegar in a bowl in the area for a day or two. The vinegar will absorb any remaining odor.

The following are some of the more common house smells and tips for eliminating them:

Cigarette Smoke. The smell of cigarette smoke is a powerful deterrent and could be an immediate deal breaker. Cigar and cigarette smoke permeates porous materials like carpets, curtains, furniture, and flooring. If you are a smoker, stop smoking in your home as soon as you decide to sell. While it may not be relaxing, smoking outdoors will help you begin to tackle the smell inside. Even in the winter, your home will need a lot of fresh air. Open a window and allow fresh air into the home daily. Thoroughly wash, steam-clean or dry-clean all surfaces, including carpets, walls, cushions, countertops, cabinetry, draperies, bedding, and upholstery. Also clean unseen areas like the edges of doors, underneath shelves and cabinets, and under appliances. Place bowls of vinegar around the house to help absorb odors. If you have years of smoke in your home, you will likely need to repaint. Prime the walls with a Kilz oil-based primer to seal the odor before you paint. For extreme cases, tear out carpeting and padding, get rid of all draperies and upholstery, clean all vents and ducts, and even clean every light bulb.

Pet Smells. Pets and their paraphernalia contribute to house smells. Make sure you clean and sanitize all litter boxes, dog kennels, pet bedding, cages, and fish tanks. Vacuum often to pick up pet hair, and wash the animal as well. If your pet has had "accidents" on the carpet, blot and clean with an enzymatic cleaner. Dry, and then sprinkle baking soda over the spot. Let it sit overnight, and vacuum the next morning. If the carpets are soiled beyond repair, replace them.

Sulfur, Rotten-Egg Smells. Clogged and slow drains can cause this type of smell, often in kitchens, bathrooms, laundry rooms, and the basement. Make sure your drains are clear and working well. Pour a blend of 1/2 cup household bleach and 1/2 cup water down the drain. Wait one hour, and then flush with lots of cold water. If the smell persists, call a plumber. In the basement, add water to the floor drain.

Musty Smells. Musty smells are most often caused by mold and mildew in damp areas. Check the house for any sources of leaks or moisture. Bathrooms and damp basements are frequently musty. Once you find where the smell is coming from, thoroughly clean the area. There are many commercial products to kill fungi, molds, and mildew. For excessively musty bathrooms, hydrochloric acid is a powerful cleaning option. However, it can damage wood, so be careful when using it. For musty basements, consider installing a dehumidifier to lower the humidity in the room and prevent the growth of bacteria and fungi. Place a bag of activated charcoal (available at home-and-garden centers or pet stores) in the basement to absorb moisture and reduce musty smells. Place the charcoal in open containers in the areas that are the dampest and darkest.

Cooking Odor. Many foods such as fish, cabbage, and fried foods leave lingering odors. Boil a teaspoon of white vinegar in one cup of water to remove unpleasant cooking odors. Get in the habit of always using your range vent when cooking. Also, try to avoid cooking strong smelling foods while your house is on the market.

Carpet Odors. If your carpets have odors, either rent a steam cleaner or hire a professional to clean them. Once dry, sprinkle baking soda over the carpet and let it sit overnight. Vacuum the following day. The baking soda will absorb odors.

Once you have the odor under control, try the following tips to keep the air fresh:

- Open windows for at least a short time every day to freshen and circulate the air. If you cannot open your windows due to the weather, turn on fans to circulate the air.

- Change dirty filters in your furnace and air conditioning unit. New filters will help trap particles that can cause odors.

- Take out the trash every day. Even if the garbage is hidden under a sink, empty it before showing the house.

- Store any smelly shoes in airtight containers or store them in the garage.

- Absorb any lingering odors by placing a few bowls of vinegar, baking soda, or kitty litter in hidden locations throughout the house (e.g, under a bed). Change these often. You can also purchase charcoal odor absorbers that do the same job.

- Just before showing your home, freshen the air by boiling a tablespoon of vinegar in a cup of water. Or, try adding 2 tablespoons of cinnamon and some orange peels to a cup of water. Boil for 10 to 15 minutes. You could also try the old trick of baking muffins or cookies immediately before a showing. Keep a bag of muffin or cookie mix on hand just to prepare before showings.

Cleaning CHECKLIST

The following are cleaning tasks required in *every* room and area of the house:

Ceilings

☐ Remove dust strings and cobwebs from ceilings and in corners.

☐ Deep clean light fixtures.

☐ Clean ceiling fans.

Walls

☐ Dust and spot clean walls.

☐ Clean light switches and switch plates.

☐ Clean baseboards.

☐ Dust all wall décor (mirrors, picture frames, etc.).

Windows

☐ Vacuum screens or remove them and hose them down outside.

☐ Clean windows, inside and out.

☐ Clean window tracks and windowsills.

☐ Clean all window treatments (blinds and draperies) according to the manufacturer's instructions.

Doors

☐ Remove all decals, stickers, nameplates, and hooks from doors.

☐ If not repainting, clean thoroughly, removing scuffmarks.

☐ Wash doorknobs and trim.

Surfaces

☐ Dust all surfaces in every room, including wood furniture, shelves, accessories, books, electronics, lampshades, etc.

☐ Steam clean upholstery.

Floors

- ☐ Vacuum or sweep floors.
- ☐ Steam clean all carpeting.
- ☐ Mop and wax or polish all other flooring.

In addition to the above, the following are extra considerations for specific rooms and areas:

Kitchen

- ☐ Clean all appliances, inside and out.
- ☐ Vacuum under and behind appliances.
- ☐ Wash the table and chairs.
- ☐ Wash the fronts of cabinets and drawers.
- ☐ Clean the undersides of hanging cabinets.
- ☐ Clean all knobs and hardware.
- ☐ Clean grout and tile.
- ☐ Wash countertops.
- ☐ Clean garbage cans, inside and out.
- ☐ Clean and polish the sink and taps.

Bathrooms

- ☐ Dust or vacuum the exhaust fan.
- ☐ Clean the tub and surrounding area, including the soap dish, showerhead, tub ledge, and corners of the tub.
- ☐ Clean all grout and tile surfaces.
- ☐ Clean the shower door.
- ☐ Clean or replace shower curtain.
- ☐ Clean the vanity.
- ☐ Clean the toilet.

Bedrooms

- Vacuum or dust the bed's headboard and footboard.
- Launder the bedspread or duvet cover and pillowcases.
- Hang duvets, blankets, or bedspreads outside in the fresh air for a few hours, if possible.
- Vacuum inside closets.

Living Room/Family Room/Dining Room

- Dust and clean wooden built-in wall units, bookshelves, and other large furniture. Use a product appropriate for the finish and type of wood.
- Dust plants.
- Dust and clean dining table and chairs and coffee tables, including the tops and legs.
- Vacuum cushions and upholstery.
- Vacuum underneath the furniture.
- If possible, steam clean upholstery or hire a professional cleaning service.
- Clean leather furniture according to manufacturer's instructions.
- Clean the fireplace.

Laundry Room:

- Wipe down the exterior of the washer and dryer.
- Vacuum behind and underneath washer and dryer, if possible.
- Clean the tops of counters or worktables.
- Clean laundry bags and hampers.

Basement/Garage:

- Sweep the floors.
- Wipe down the furnace and water heater.
- Change the filters in the furnace and air conditioning unit.

- [ ] Refill floor drain in the basement, if required.
- [ ] Reduce mustiness in the basement with a dehumidifier, if necessary.
- [ ] Clean and sanitize all litter boxes, dog kennels, pet bedding, cages, and fish tanks.

chapter six

Step 4: Styling

POTENTIAL BUYERS WON'T MAKE AN OFFER if they can't remember your house or differentiate it from other listings. According to the TD Canada Trust 2010 Home Buyers Report, the average home buyer visits more than 15 houses and looks at countless others online before making a purchase. A house that is "mediocre," "ok," or "average" isn't a hot seller because it isn't memorable. You need to make your house stand out from the competition and make buyers remember it (in a good way).

Author and columnist Malcolm Gladwell has a theory called "the stickiness factor" that resonates with home staging. He says that for a message or product to be successful, it must be memorable (i.e., "sticky"), and a product that is memorable enough will spur people to action. He suggests that marketers can improve a product's stickiness simply by tinkering with its presentation in small and subtle ways. People remember houses that are visually attractive to them. By making small and sometimes subtle changes to how you style your home (e.g., the presentation of furniture, art, and accessories), you can dramatically improve its "stickiness," encouraging buyers to notice it, remember it, and make an offer.

The fourth step to staging your home is styling it, which involves creating focal points; rearranging your furniture; choosing appropriate lighting, art, and accessories; and displaying creative vignettes. Proper styling will make your house pleasing to almost anyone's tastes.

Principles Of Styling Your Home

"It's hard to believe how much more appealing a home can be once it has been staged. By simply removing some tired, old items and adding some tasteful touches, staging managed to turn what was a rather ordinary space into something beautiful, comfortable and inviting."

Pauline Beres, homeowner

The following are a few general principles to remember before you begin styling your house:

- **Forget about perfection.** Don't think that your house has to be exquisitely decorated to get the right kind of attention and attract the most buyers. You don't have to be a decorating diva or have expensive furniture and accessories to stage your home. In fact, houses that are too perfectly decorated can actually turn away buyers. In a perfectly decorated home, potential buyers might focus on all the beautiful things in the house rather than on the house itself; they may even decide that the house is only appealing *because* of these beautiful things. They may also feel intimidated by a beautifully furnished room and have trouble imagining their belongings in such a luxurious place. If people can't imagine themselves or their belongings in the house, they are unlikely to buy it. Most people aren't looking for a perfectly decorated home; they're looking for a well-maintained home to which they feel a connection.

- **Avoid decorating extremes.** Stay away from creating a particular style or theme in a room. For example, you may love French colonial décor in your living room and your kids may love their "under the sea" themed bathroom, but potential buyers may not. Why limit the pool of potential buyers to only those who share your taste? It's better to style your house with neutral décor so that it appeals to as wide a market as possible. By neutral décor, we mean a look that has no identifiable style and is simple, classic, and elegant. Avoid décor that is too eye-catching, distinctive, cutesy, or distracting. The best way to showcase the room is to style it so that the items in the room highlight the space rather than compete with it.

- **Arrange furnishings and accessories to make the room appear as spacious as possible.** After de-cluttering, you probably felt that the room seemed lighter, airier, and bigger. Organizing your furniture and accessories to highlight focal points and create clear sight lines through a room will further improve its perceived spaciousness.

- **Style your home so that it appears as light and bright as possible.** A bright room is cheery, comfortable, and puts buyers at ease. In other words, light sells. Harness the power of natural and artificial light to make your home attractive to buyers.

- **Use art and accessories to add colour and personality to the room.** A room that is perfectly de-cluttered, depersonalized, and clean would be cold and sterile without some decorative elements. Some colour and warmth is absolutely necessary for buyers to form an emotional connection with the place, and these elements are added through art and accessories.

Focal Points

Every room in your home needs a *focal point*—a place that draws attention and adds interest to the room. It's usually the most obvious feature in a room and is the first thing that captures attention. Make sure that it is also the best feature of the room.

When buyers' eyes are drawn to a desirable focal point, they are not as likely to notice undesirable elements, such as worn carpeting. Of course, we don't recommend you hide problems, but part of the magic of home staging is that it highlights a house's strengths and downplays its weaknesses. Showcasing desirable features is a key strategy to creating positive impressions of your house.

Creating Focal Points

To choose a focal point, see where your eye naturally falls when you enter the room. Also consider what you wish to feature in the room. If the existing focal point is not ideal, you may need to highlight something else. Ideally, it should be a permanent feature of the house. For example, a large window, a kitchen island, or built-in cabinets are good choices because they are desirable features that will help sell the house.

A room should have only one focal point; having more than one divides the viewer's attention and causes confusion. For example, many family rooms have three prominent features: a TV, window, and fireplace. In this case, highlight the most valuable fixed feature of the room, which in this case, is either the fireplace or the window. To decide which of the two to highlight, ask yourself whether the fireplace or window would most interest buyers. Which is easier to highlight? Is the view out of the window a good one? Is the fireplace attractive or has it seen better days?

If a room doesn't have an attractive fixed feature, use a belonging as a focal point, such as a lovely picture, brightly coloured toss cushions, or a tasteful display of fresh flowers. In many homes, a big-screen TV is the most prominent feature of the family room, or there is a TV hanging over the fireplace and the two are one visual unit. Although most decorators wouldn't choose to have a TV as the focal point, it might intrigue buyers when they see the room is spacious enough for their (possibly future) big-screen TV. Unless you want to remove your big-screen TV, use it as the focal point.

Once you decide on the focal point, make the most of it by arranging furniture and accessories to direct attention to it. Place furniture around the feature and try to place the sofa so that it faces it. For example, if the focal point is a fireplace, position furniture so that the chairs frame it. Hang a picture or a mirror over the mantel, and add a few well-chosen accessories on either or both ends of the mantel. These touches will showcase the fireplace as a valuable feature of the room.

Filling a Corner

When you walk into a room, your eye will most often naturally fall to the far corner of the room. Give it a try. Walk into a bedroom in your home and see where you first look. Chances are that you cast your gaze on the corner furthest from the door. This, however, isn't always the area of a room that you want to highlight. Although the intent is not to make this corner the focal point, you can soften it and add visual interest by placing a tall plant, lamp, or a vase filled with branches in this corner. Then choose a desirable fixed feature in the room as a focal point.

In this kitchen, the focal point is the beautiful, large window. Red flowers, glass bottles, and tea towel add a punch of colour and guide visitors' eyes to the window.

Furniture Placement

In chapter 3, we advised removing extra furniture and furniture that is too large for the room. Take another look now and make sure that you were ruthless. Observe the adage "less is more" as you strip the room down to its essentials.

Be aware that you might need to remove your favourite chair. Accept the idea that you may not be as comfortable in the room after it's staged. How you stage the room may not be the way you would choose to live in it. Your goal is to please buyers, not necessarily yourself. Staging a room to make it seem bigger will attract buyer interest.

Aim to leave plenty of empty floor space to improve traffic flow and increase the feeling of spaciousness. In major traffic areas have a clear, straight path about 3½-feet wide through the room. (However, make sure this path doesn't cross in front of the focal point.) As a general guide, also try to leave the following spaces unobstructed:

- 2 to 3 feet between sofas and chairs in conversation areas.
- 18 inches between a coffee table and sofa.
- 3 feet between the edge of the dining room table and the wall.
- At least 2 feet between the side of the bed and the wall.
- 3½ feet between the bed and a dresser.

A Word About Furniture

You don't need new, expensive furniture to sell your house. If your furniture is a neutral colour and is in good condition, it may just need a thorough vacuuming and steam cleaning to revive it. Add some toss cushions and a throw to dress it up.

If your furniture is worn, outdated, has a distracting colour, or is too large for the room, consider storing it and renting more appropriate furniture from a professional stager or a rental store. The rates are usually reasonable, considering the dramatic improvement to the room's presentation. You can also rent end tables and accessories if necessary.

Of course, if you're planning on buying furniture for your new place, consider buying it early and using it to stage your house.

The following are some general tips on furniture placement:

- To save on heavy lifting, first plan where you want to move your furniture. Sketch a simple diagram of the room and cut out representations of your furniture. Place the cutouts in various arrangements on your diagram until you find one that works.
- Place the largest piece of furniture along the longest wall.
- Place sofas and chairs facing one another to create a conversation grouping.
- In large rooms, create more than one conversation area by arranging groups of furniture.
- Avoid lining all the furniture around the four walls of the room, leaving an empty space in the middle; group the furniture closer together. If furniture must be against a wall, pull it out at least a couple inches.
- Try to place the sofa facing the focal point.
- Try placing a piece of furniture—such as a sofa, dresser, or chair—at an angle in a corner to create more space, soften the corner, and improve traffic flow.

- Move the largest pieces of furniture opposite to the room's entrance, if possible. Buyers' eyes will be drawn to the larger piece, creating the illusion of extra depth and space.

- Keep the quantity and size of furniture and accessories the same on both sides of the room. If one side of the room attracts more of your attention than the other, then the room isn't balanced and you should rearrange it.

- Keep doorways and entranceways clear. Doors should be able to open fully without bumping into anything.

- Remove furniture from hallways and stairwell landings to open up these cramped spaces.

- Use neutral-coloured area rugs to anchor and warm a seating area. Don't lay a small rug under the coffee table; use a rug large enough to accommodate at least the front legs of all surrounding furniture. If using a very large rug, make sure it leaves at least 2 feet of open space around the perimeter of the room. In a dining room, use a rug that is large enough for the chairs to be pulled out without going over the rug's edge.

- In bedrooms, place the headboard on the longest wall, opposite the door. Avoid placing the bed on the same wall as the door; the bed is the focal point so you should see it as you walk in the room.

It's easier to move heavy pieces of furniture on hardwood, laminate, cork, or tile flooring if you place rags or towels under the legs of the furniture and carefully slide the furniture into place with assistance from a helper. You can also buy felt- or plastic-covered furniture slides that enable one person to easily move heavy furniture over hard flooring or carpeting. Just tilt the furniture and place a slide under each corner and then push or pull the item. Remember to sweep hard floors before moving furniture to prevent scratches.

Play around with the placement of furniture until you find a layout that is pleasing to you. Once your furniture is in place, leave the room and come back several times. Keep moving the furniture until it seems right.

Lighting

A dark, dreary room is a major buyer deterrent, whereas a bright, cheery room is a strong selling point. When styling a room, therefore, try to make it as light and bright as possible.

Natural Light

The ideal source of light for any room is abundant natural light. It makes the room feel more welcoming, spacious, and comfortable. The most prized light sources, therefore, are windows. Make sure they're sparkling clean inside and out to let in as much light as possible. If you don't usually open the window, and especially if it's a focal point, consider removing the screen to improve the view and further brighten the room.

Keep windows unobstructed to increase the amount of sunlight allowed in. Remove everything off the windows and the sills, such as potted plants, stickers, sun catchers, or wind chimes. Also remove objects placed in front of the window; they block the sunlight and distract from the view.

Check that nothing outside is blocking the window, such as overgrown shrubs or cedars. Ruthlessly trim, cut back, or remove these.

If privacy isn't an issue, consider taking down window coverings, especially in small rooms. Removing window coverings will not only brighten the room, it will also showcase the window and make the room feel larger.

If privacy is an issue and you need window coverings, remember to pull back curtains and raise blinds before photographing or showing the house. Ensure curtains and side panels cover as little of the windowpane as possible. They should hang so that the inside edge is even with the inside window casing. Sheer curtains offer privacy without being too overpowering, but again, pull these back for showings and pictures. (Choosing window coverings is discussed later in this chapter.)

Artificial Light

Living areas need a variety of artificial lighting to warm the space and create an inviting atmosphere. Most rooms benefit from having both ambient and task lighting. Accent lighting can also be used to highlight special features.

- **Ambient lighting** is the major artificial lighting in the room and is usually wired into the house during construction. Examples include ceiling lights, chandeliers, and recessed lights. Chapter 4 discusses tips for updating and hanging light fixtures.

- **Task lighting** directs light to a particular area where it's needed to perform a task (such as reading, writing, or cooking). Lamps and under-cabinet lighting are examples. Try to include about three lamps (including table and floor lamps) in the living/family room and place them in a triangular pattern around the room to bounce light off the ceilings and walls. Choose simple lamps with neutral-coloured shades. For lighting under cabinets or counters, you can install battery-operated lights that adhere to the underside of the cabinet and give a nice glow for evening showings.

- **Accent lighting** highlights a particular feature or accessory, such as a piece of art or a fireplace, creating drama and interest in a room.

Illuminating Math

In general, try to have about 1.5 watts of lighting for every square foot of floor space. To determine the correct wattage for a room, multiply the length and width of the room in feet, and then multiple that product by 1.5. Example: For a 10 x 12 room, multiply the dimensions (10 x 12 = 120), and then multiply that product by 1.5 (120 x 1.5 = 180). Total illumination needed for that room, therefore, is 180 watts.

In a specific work area (e.g., over the kitchen island), try to have about 2.5 watts of light for every square foot. Therefore, multiply the length (in feet) by the width of the work area and then multiple that product by 2.5. Example: For a 4 x 6 foot island, multiply the dimensions (4 x 6 = 24) and then multiply by 2.5 (24 x 2.5 = 60). Total illumination required is at least 60 watts in this work area.

For all lamps and fixtures, maximize light by using the highest wattage recommended for the fixture. In particularly dark or north-facing rooms, choose full-spectrum bulbs for a more natural-looking light. Also choose the right bulbs for your fixtures. When fixtures are clear glass or have exposed bulbs, select clear bulbs. Fixtures or lamps with linen shades and frosted bulbs will cast a soft, pleasing glow.

Art

Whether it's a focal point, accent, or simply part of the background, art is an important element in a room. You can style your home using a wide variety of artwork, such as framed paintings, photos, prints, clocks, mirrors, and wooden or metal wall hangings.

As tempting as it may be, resist the urge to cover every wall with a piece of art. Include just a few select pieces for each room, and leave at least one empty wall in each room. Too many wall hangings make the room look cluttered, whereas an empty wall increases the sense of spaciousness and invites potential buyers to imagine their art hanging there.

To select the best artwork for each room, consider the following:

- **Theme.** Landscapes and abstracts are inoffensive and non-controversial, making them perfect choices for staging your home. Avoid pieces that are gimmicky or over the top, such as a moving waterfall picture. The art should enhance the room, not dominate it.

- **Colour.** The main colours in the art should complement, but not necessarily match, the colours of the wall, floor, and furnishings. Also make sure the colour and material of the frame also suit the room.

- **Size.** Choose artwork that is in scale with its surroundings. For example, don't place a small piece of art on a large expanse of wall; the art will look lost. Likewise, don't place a large piece of art on a small wall; the art will dominate the space.

You don't have to have expensive artwork to stage your home. Simply choose something that's the right theme, colour, and size to help ground the space. Pier One, Ikea, Home Sense, and many other stores have a wide selection of affordable, framed art that would be appropriate. You could also purchase inexpensive frames to use for posters, prints, or even samples of graphic wallpaper, wrapping paper, or scrapbooking paper.

Display framed photographs as long as they aren't too personal; choose pictures that feature landscapes or activities, for example, rather than weddings, graduation, or family portraits. A popular option is having a photograph printed onto canvas and then stretched onto a wooden frame; the finished product has the texture and depth of a painting. Create any size that you want, and simply hang it unframed. You can order a canvas photograph online through Canvascanada.ca, Blacks.ca, or a local camera store.

Using Mirrors as Wall Art

Not sure about what picture to hang? Consider hanging a mirror instead. Research suggests that customers stay longer in stores where they can see themselves in mirrors. The same may be true for people viewing houses.

Mirrors add dimension, and by reflecting light or a great view they can make the room seem brighter and more spacious. The size, shape, and style of the mirror and frame contribute to its impact.

If you want a mirror to be the focal point in your room, choose one that is large enough to command attention and has an eye-catching frame. You could lean an oversized mirror against the wall, rather than hang it. To make sure no one knocks it over, secure it with a wall mount safety bracket. Try hanging a mirror framed like a window to create the illusion of a window. However you hang your mirror, make sure it reflects natural light or an appealing view.

Hanging Art

Once you've chosen your pieces, decide where to display them. Hang art where it can relate to something nearby, such as over a fireplace or sofa or near a chair or table.

When hanging art over a fireplace, make sure it is about two-thirds the width of the mantel. The piece shouldn't be wider than the mantel or less than half of the mantel's width. Likewise, when hanging art over a sofa or other piece of furniture, choose pieces that are about two-thirds of the width of the furniture beneath it. Centre the art directly over the fireplace or furniture.

In this living room, a few pieces of art make a strong impact. The framed picture over the fireplace draws attention to this selling feature and adds subtle colour. Also notice how the two mirrors leaning against the walls beside the fireplace expand the room and add dimension to otherwise empty spaces.

If you're hanging art without anything underneath it, centre it between two distinct points. For example, on a long wall, a piece of art may be centred between a plant and a corner of the room. Or it may be centred between a chair and a shelf. The "two-thirds rule" still applies. Choose a piece that fills approximately two-thirds of the space between the two points.

Also match the shape of the art to the shape of the wall. For walls that are narrow, hang a tall, vertical piece to accentuate the height. To accentuate a wide space, hang a long, horizontal piece. However, to avoid a cluttered look, don't hang art on walls less than two-feet wide.

People usually hang artwork too high. When hanging art above a mantle or piece of furniture, position it so that the bottom of the frame is about 6 to 8 inches above the top of the mantel or furniture. If there is no furniture under the picture, hang the art so that its centre is about 5 feet from the floor (i.e., at eye level). Hang pictures a little lower in areas where people will usually be seated (such as in a dining room or near a chair).

The art in this photo is centred between the vase and the chair, filling approximately two-thirds of the space between the two. It is hanging at eye-level to a person sitting in the chair.

Creating Groupings of Artwork

If you don't have a large piece of art, you can group smaller pieces; these act as one unit and together they can achieve the proper width. Make sure that the size of the grouping is about two-thirds the width of the object below and that bottoms of the frames are about 6 to 8 inches above the top of the furniture. Whether you simply align two pieces side by side or arrange several small items together for a gallery effect, use your creativity to design an attractive and interesting look.

Consider a theme for your grouping, or group pieces that are similar in colour or material. Similarly coloured frames and matting will unify the grouping and create a smart look.

Protecting the Wall

If you haven't painted the walls recently and you want to reposition artwork, you might have nail holes and marred walls to contend with. If necessary, fill nail holes, touch up the paint, and try to gently remove scuffmarks left by the frames. Add adhesive gel tabs or small pieces of felt onto the back corners of frames to protect the walls. If the piece of art is lightweight, try mounting it with 3M Command picture-hanging strips. One strip adheres to the wall and other adheres to the picture, and they stick together like Velcro. The strips are easy to remove and don't mark the wall.

If you have an even number of pictures that are about the same size, line them up to form a square or rectangle, with their edges even. You can be less precise when hanging different sized pictures in a group. For these, pick a centre point on the wall and imagine a horizontal and a vertical line crossing through it. Hang the pictures roughly equal space above, below, and on either side of the lines. The edges don't need to match, and don't worry about having equal spacing between the pieces. Just try different arrangements until you're satisfied with the look.

Before hammering in nails, lay the pictures on the floor and work with them there until you find a pleasing pattern. You could also trace the shape of each piece onto paper, cut out the shapes, and hang them on the wall with sticky tack or painter's tape. Once you're satisfied with their positions, insert the hangers over the paper and then remove the paper. Your pictures are now ready to hang.

Accessories

Accessories are like the jewelry of the room; they finish the room by adding interest, colour, and a touch of personality. Without losing your neutral and uncluttered look, add the right amount and types of accessories to create a look of stylish elegance and a pop of colour. Used correctly, accessories will complement the design of the house and help to make it truly memorable.

If you had set aside a box of accessories while you were de-cluttering your house, sort through them and choose some to display, remembering the adage "less is more." Too many accessories will compete with each other for attention, leaving buyers overwhelmed and distracted.

If you don't have enough accessories or you're not satisfied with what you have, you may need to purchase a few items. Because the best accessories for home staging tend to be classic items, anything you buy to stage your house will probably also work well in your new home.

No-Fail Accessories

Certain types of accessories always improve the look of a room. Generally, the best accessories appeal to more than one of the senses. For example, a beeswax candle looks attractive and naturally smells lovely. A cream-coloured knit throw draped across a dark leather couch adds colour and texture. A bowl of green apples on a kitchen countertop looks attractive and delectable.

Our favorite no-fail accessories include the following:

- **Fruit.** Whether it's fresh or faux (good quality, of course), fruit displayed in a bowl or basket adds a lively splash of colour and makes the room look lived in. Choose fruit with bold colours that complement those in the room, such as bright lemons or limes, green apples, or crimson pomegranates.

- **Candles.** Candles add simple elegance and a warm ambiance, even when they're unlit. (For safety, don't light candles when showing your home.) Arrange candles in small clusters and stagger their heights. For a more lived-in look, light and then blow out a brand-new candle so that the wick is blackened. To mimic the light and ambiance of a lit candle, try using candles or tea lights with battery-operated flames.

- **Books.** Books are essential staging props that easily fill an empty corner or create a cozy and inviting scene. Of course, consider the titles of the books, and avoid using any that could be considered offensive or controversial. Use books with neutral subjects or classics. Display books that are similar in size and complementary in colour. Coffee table and hard-covered books are ideal. If the book is too colourful, remove the dust jacket. Add height and interest to an end table or shelf by displaying some books standing on their ends and others stacked flat. Remember not to overdo it: display only a few books to add a spot of colour or some visual weight. You can also display magazines with attractive covers, such as home décor, architecture, or nature magazines. Coordinate the colour of the cover of the magazine with the room colours.

- **Fresh flowers.** Nothing livens up a room like fresh flowers. The vase doesn't have to be fancy. An old mason jar looks lovely holding a bouquet of fresh flowers. Carla Scharback, owner of Blossoms Living, suggests using large cymbidium, orchids, or spider chrysanthemums for home staging. She also favors flowering branches or tropical leaves in large vases. If these varieties aren't available, simply purchase an affordable bunch (no carnations) from your grocery store and arrange them yourself. Choose a single variety of flowers in a neutral colour that will blend with your décor. White- or cream-coloured flowers are ideal. Add lots of greenery to your arrangement. Another economical option is to buy several simple, narrow clear glass vases (check your local dollar store) and add single blooms with a sprig of greenery. A single orchid in the entry way provides a stunning welcome.

- **Healthy plants or silk plants.** Use plants to fill in bare spots or as simple additions in areas that need a little something more. Shun anything that looks sick, cuttings in a glass jar, and plants that climb to the ceiling or desperately lean toward a light source. Go to your local grocery store and pick a few healthy looking plants that you can pop into pretty pots. Take good care of them during the time you home is on the market. Keep a lush group of sun-loving plants by a sunny window where they'll thrive, and then move them to a north-facing room to enliven the space. You can also display tropical or exotic silk plants, but make sure they are clean and look authentic.

- **Fabrics and linens.** Fabric should be present in every room to add layers of colour, depth, and softness. Vary the types of textures by mixing cottons, chenille, wool, linens, and even velvet. Fabric accessories include accent pillows, throws, window side panels, bedding, towels, and even tea towels. Add accent pillows to your sofas, chairs, and even on your bed. For bathroom towels, purchase a new set for display, and set them aside after showings so they're always clean and ready for the next showing. Replace old or unattractive bedding to style the bedrooms. Choose bedding that is neutral coloured (browns, beiges, whites, and creams work well), has minimal pattern, and has coordinating bed skirt and shams. GlucksteinHome and Steven & Chris linens are excellent and are available at Home Outfitters and The Bay. Reputable online shopping sites that ship linens to Canada include Heirloomlinens.com, Downunderbedding.com, Potterybarn.ca, and Ikea.ca. A lower cost option is to buy a bed-in-a-bag package from Winners, Home Sense, or Walmart.

- **Vases or Bowls.** A decorative vase or bowl can be used to display anything from flowers or branches to fruits or decorative ornaments. It can also be displayed empty for a simple look, such as on a mantel or near a picture.

- **Trays.** Trays are useful for displaying a small group of candles or smaller accessories. Grouping these together on a tray gives a cohesive look.

- **Mirrors, crystal, glass and shiny surfaces.** Mirrors and glass add dimension and sparkle to a home. Add a mirror at your front entrance. Place a candle on a small mirror or reflective plate and place on a table. Display a large glass or crystal bowl on your kitchen counter. Make sure every room has some shine.

A small mirror, glass detailing on the lamp, and a shiny accessory make this bedside table sparkle.

Photo by Hans Holtkamp

Folding Towels

To make hanging hand and bath towels look full and luxurious, use a "hotel fold":

1. Lay the towel upside down, with the tag facing up.

2. With the short edge near you, take the right side and fold it into the middle point.

3. Take the left side and fold it over top of the first fold, covering it completely.

4. Pick up the towel and fold it in half.

Hang the towel on the bar so that no edges show and the decorative edging is displayed.

To display a plush stack of towels on the edge of a soaker tub or on a shelf, follow the directions above and then fold the towel in half again. Stack three or more towels so that the folded sides are facing the front. You could also simply set out one folded towel and place a new decorative soap, loofah, or wooden bath brush on top.

Accessorizing with Window Treatments

To create a fresh and updated look, remove outdated or "busy" window coverings, such as heavy draperies, plastic or vertical blinds, tab topped drapes, swags, and pleated, ruffled, or balloon valances. For staging purposes, your house may look just fine without any window coverings.

If you need blinds for privacy, Christine Korchinski of Christine's Drapery suggests installing a two-inch faux wood Venetian in a neutral colour. These are reasonably priced and will update your home beautifully.

If your living room or master bedroom needs some extra colour and texture, consider installing a decorative rod and side panels, which are stationary panels of fabric hanging at the sides of the window. Side panels also give the illusion of a wider window.

Choose side panels that blend in with the wall colour to add texture without being distracting. If you want to draw attention to the window or view, choose side panels in a colour that complements the accent colours in the room (such as the colours in the rug or throw cushions).

Creating Drama With Accessories

Once you decide which accessories to use, display them to create simple but dramatic arrangements, keeping in mind the accessory's colour, size, and placement.

Colour. Accessories are an ideal way to introduce colour into a neutral room. Choose one accent colour and use it sparingly. Pick a colour that already exists in small amounts in a piece of art, furniture, or flooring, and then repeat this colour in small doses around the room. For example, the accent colour may appear in the art, in pillows, on a vase on the mantel, and on book spines displayed on a shelf. Try to have the colour appear on several levels throughout the room: at eye level, table level, and floor level.

Pockets of colour help to guide the eye around the room. Buyers will immediately be drawn to the accent colour and then move around to each piece with that colour, taking in and enjoying all the details of the room.

A bold blast of colour draws attention and creates energy. Red, orange, yellow, and lime green are excellent bold accent colours because they add a snap of the unexpected. Use a bold colour to draw attention to features that you want buyers to notice. For example, a painting with red accents hanging over a fireplace will draw the eye to this feature. Likewise, a bowl of lemons or red apples displayed on a kitchen countertop will showcase it.

Accessories don't have to be bold coloured to be effective: soft, understated colours, such as muted blues and greens, blend in with the room to create a calming, peaceful environment. Because they recede into the room rather than stand out, they also create an open and airy feeling, which helps to make the room feel more spacious.

Ideally, accessorize the rooms in your house to create both quiet, calming rooms (such as bedrooms, bathrooms) and energetic rooms (such as the kitchen and living rooms).

Size. The size of an accessory is an important consideration, especially when grouping them together. Here are some general principles about size:

- Go bigger than you think you need for most accessories, including pillows and vases.
- Make sure the size of the accessories is proportionate to the size of the surface on which they are placed. In some cases, consider the size

of a portion of the surface rather than the entire surface. For example, when placing a vase on a mantel next to a picture, the visual space is the area between the edge of the mantel and the edge of the frame, not the entire mantel. Therefore, choose a vase or group of items that occupy roughly one- to two-thirds of this area.

- Make sure the smallest item in a grouping is at least two-thirds the size of the largest item. Pairing one item with another half its size looks unbalanced.

- Vary the heights of items displayed in a grouping (i.e., small, medium, and large), but don't line them up in order of size. Create depth by layering items, staggering them one in front of the other. Display the grouping on a pretty plate or tray.

Placement. When placing accessories, play around until it looks just right; moving them around even a few inches here or there can make a difference. Also consider the following:

- Keep it simple. Many people display too many accessories, reducing their impact and making the room cluttered. Display single items of larger pieces, and three or five smaller items in a group. (An odd-numbered group of items is more pleasing to the eye than an even-numbered group.)

- Group together accessories that match or are alike in theme. Different objects of the same colour can look pleasing together—coordinating colours is the key here.

- Display accessories on mantels that pick up on the theme and colour of the art hanging above the fireplace. Consider using tall items in scale with the height of the fireplace, such as a vase of branches or tall flowers. Don't be too symmetrical; both sides of the mantel don't have to match. You might want to put one object on one side and three on the other, or one on one side and nothing on the other.

There are too many accessories in this room and most of them are too small for the space. Another problem is that the picture is hanging too high over the mantel.

After de-cluttering the shelves and mantel and hanging a larger picture closer to the mantel, the room is now elegantly styled. A touch of red helps to energize the room.

Styling Bookcases and Shelves

Give extra consideration to shelves when styling. Create interest in the room by displaying more than just books:

- Empty the bookshelf and then sort books according to the predominant colour of the book jacket. Use only the black, brown, tan, white and cream-coloured books. Pack the rest.

- Working in a zig-zag pattern down the shelves, replace the books. Stand some upright, and lay some down flat. When stacking books, place the biggest books on the bottom and the smallest on the top.

- Leave room to display items other than books, such as small boxes, figurines, candles, a small potted or silk plant, or small pieces of art. Use contrasting shapes and textures, and keep the colours subtle.
- Fill only two-thirds of the available space.
- Vary the heights of accessories and books. Create highs and lows on each shelf.
- Create layers. For example, a small dish in front of a picture adds depth.
- Place heaviest looking books or objects on the bottom shelves.

Vignettes

Professional home stagers usually include one last styling element that appeals to buyers' emotions and makes the house memorable: a vignette.

A vignette is an arrangement of furniture or accessories that essentially tells a story about the house and lifestyle of those living in it. For example, setting the dining room table with dinnerware and a centerpiece as if waiting for dinner guests. Or placing stools at the kitchen island along with a tray of glasses, as if ready for a casual gathering. Both send a message: the dining room says that the house is perfect for formal entertaining, and the staged island shows that the kitchen is a place where friends can gather and relax.

A simple vignette in the kitchen makes a comforting scene.

Vignettes are optional and should be used sparingly. Only include one or two vignettes to avoid having the house look too staged. Used appropriately, vignettes add charm and interest. Use your imagination to create scenes that set the mood or tell a story. You can get ideas from home decorating magazines or even furniture showrooms.

Every space in and around your home provides an opportunity to communicate that your home is a great place to live. The following are some ideas to get you started:

- On the porch or deck, set out two wicker chairs and a small table between them, with a large pitcher of iced tea and two glasses sitting on the table.

- In the living or family room, create a cozy reading corner, complete with a book left open and a coffee mug beside it.

- In the kitchen, set out a clean wooden cutting board and place a few fresh tomatoes and a couple of pretty oil and vinegar bottles.

- In the dining room, set the table with placemats, plates, and glassware (no flatware). Include a centerpiece of fresh flowers, a unique candleholder, or a nice vase. Only use a tablecloth if the table is in poor shape, but make sure the tablecloth is a muted colour. James Rayner of Cava Secreta suggests using white tableware and accenting with bold-coloured water glasses that fit the colour theme of the house. Use no more than three pieces of stemware per setting, and use the tallest stemware possible for a dramatic effect.

- In a child's bedroom, place a few stuffed toys on the bed and dresser, complementing the colours in the room.

- In a basement family room, display a board game in progress or a partially completed puzzle; if you have a pool table, rack the balls and leave a cue lying across the table, as if you're ready to begin a game.

- In the master bathroom, create a spa feeling by including a basket with an assortment of fancy soaps, bath beads, and a bottle of bath oil or lotion.

Home Styling CHECKLIST

Front Entrance

☐ Make a clear traffic path from the front door to the rest of the house.

☐ Include a small table and a chair or bench if there's space.

☐ Display a new, good quality mat. Match the rug to the floor so that the flooring stands out, not the rug. Use a mat that is large enough to fill the space and expose at least nine inches of floor around it.

☐ Consider adding accent lighting, such as a small lamp on the table.

☐ Hang a framed picture or mirror on a large blank wall.

☐ Place a small plant or vase of fresh flowers on the table.

Kitchen

☐ Choose a focal point and highlight this feature using accessories (e.g., a vase of flowers on the island or a bowl of lemons on the counter).

☐ Ensure there's a clear traffic path through the kitchen to the adjoining rooms.

☐ Remove window coverings and/or valences.

☐ Clear the windowsill.

☐ Remove anything hanging on or near the window (e.g., sun catcher, hanging plant).

☐ Leave three attractive items on the counter, such as an espresso machine or high-end coffee maker, an attractive cookbook opened on a stand, small potted plants, or a decorative cookie jar. Do not display more than one appliance.

☐ Use wall art sparingly; leave most of the walls bare in a small kitchen.

☐ Ensure there's enough task lighting. Consider adding wireless, stick-on lighting under the cabinets if needed.

Dining Room

☐ Centre the table under the chandelier.

☐ Keep only four chairs at the table, unless the room is very large. For a rectangular table, place two chairs on each side of the table, with no chairs on either end of the table. (Remove extra leaves to make the table as small as possible.)

- ☐ Push the chairs completely in and under the table.
- ☐ Set the table with a centerpiece, placemats, plates, and glassware (no flatware).
- ☐ Display accessories on the sideboard, if there is one.
- ☐ Hang wall décor over the sideboard, if appropriate.
- ☐ Display a few select pieces in a china cabinet. Leave the shelves at least one-third to one-half empty.
- ☐ Remove outdated or "busy" window coverings. If privacy is an issue, replace with simple venetian blinds or sheer curtains. Consider adding side panels in a neutral colour to soften the window.
- ☐ Include another source of lighting to complement the chandelier, such as a lamp to brighten a dark corner.

Main Living Areas
(Living Room, Family Room, or Great Room)

- ☐ Choose a focal point that is a selling feature if possible; arrange furniture around or facing it and add colour and accessories near or on it.
- ☐ Ensure furniture is clean and in good repair; if necessary, borrow, rent, or buy new furniture that you can use in your new place. Furniture should be neutral coloured with minimal patterning.
- ☐ Pull furniture away from the walls and arrange into a conversation grouping if there's space.
- ☐ Remove anything blocking windows (e.g., plants) or doorways (e.g., furniture). Keep a good line of sight through the windows and a free pathway through the doors and through the room.
- ☐ Ensure there is adequate lighting; have two or three lamps with white or cream shades.
- ☐ Remove window coverings if privacy isn't an issue.
- ☐ Remove outdated or "busy" window coverings. If privacy is an issue,

replace with neutral-coloured venetian blinds or sheer curtains. Consider adding simple side panels in a neutral colour to soften the window.

- ☐ Hang artwork or a framed mirror above the fireplace mantel; art should be about two-thirds the width of the mantel.
- ☐ Hang art over the sofa if the sofa is along a long wall; art should be about two-thirds the width of the sofa.
- ☐ Hang art 6 to 8 inches above the top of the furniture or fireplace mantel, or hang it so its middle is about 5 feet from the floor (i.e., at eye level).
- ☐ Make sure art isn't placed too high.
- ☐ Repeat the same accent colour a few places throughout the room.
- ☐ Accessorize the fireplace mantel. Display tall accessories on the mantle.
- ☐ Add a new area rug (neutral colour and solid design), throw cushions, and accessories, if required.
- ☐ Add a large, leafy plant in an empty corner and fresh flowers on a table.
- ☐ Style shelves or bookcases with books, art, and accessories.

Bathrooms

- ☐ Remove garbage bin, or place out of sight in a cupboard or closet.
- ☐ Hang a fresh, neutral-coloured fabric shower curtain (white or cream); include a new vinyl liner behind the curtain.
- ☐ Hang a picture above the toilet, about 16 inches above the tank.
- ☐ Display only a soap pump and a small vase of fresh greenery on the vanity top.
- ☐ Hang fresh, coordinating bath and hand towels for showing your home. Thick white towels give a spa-like feeling to the room. Drape folded bath towels (hotel fold) over the towel bar, and hang a folded hand towel over each bath towel to create layers.
- ☐ If space permits, include a small display near a soaker tub, such as a basket of decorative soaps, a vase of branches, or a stack of folded towels.

Bedrooms

- ☐ Move the bed to the wall opposite the door so that it is the first object seen when entering the room.

- ☐ Remove the TV.

- ☐ Place a small nightstand on one or both sides of the bed.

- ☐ Keep items on the nightstand to a minimum.

- ☐ Ensure bedding is clean and a neutral colour.

- ☐ Place throw pillows in a coordinating accent colour on the bed.

- ☐ Repeat the same accent colour a few places throughout the room.

- ☐ Use a bed skirt if you're storing items under the bed.

- ☐ Remove outdated or "busy" window coverings. Replace with blinds or sheer curtains. Consider adding side panels in a neutral colour.

- ☐ Hang wall art; over the bed is usually an ideal place.

Hallways and Stairwells

- ☐ Keep the walls bare and the stairs clear.

- ☐ Keep hallways furniture-free.

Laundry Room

- ☐ Remove throw rug.

- ☐ Put detergent in an apothecary jar with a scoop and display on top of washing machine, or set a stack of nicely folded white towels on top of the machine.

PART THREE

Almost Showtime!

This section addresses some final, yet essential, staging considerations: how to create sensational curb appeal; what to do when you need to sell a vacant property and other special cases; and how to photograph, maintain, and show your staged house. By the end of this section, you'll be more than ready to welcome potential buyers in and impress them with your beautiful home.

chapter seven

Curb Appeal

PREPARING YOUR HOUSE FOR SALE isn't limited to only staging the interior. To present a truly exceptional listing, you also have to consider how your house looks on the outside. "Curb appeal" refers to how your house looks from potential buyers' first vantage point: the curbside. Good curb appeal is essential because it shows buyers what to expect on the inside.

Whether viewing photos online, arriving at the house for the first time in person, or just driving by, potential buyers see the exterior first. What they see here significantly influences whether they decide to look inside. It takes only seconds for a potential buyer to form strong opinions of a house—how well it's maintained, how clean it is, its perceived value, and what it's probably like inside—all based on a mere glance of the outside of the house and the yard.

Remember, people form quick, intuitive judgments based on what they see, and their first opinion about a house is very important. By investing a little time and effort into improving your home's curb appeal, you'll draw buyers in. Don't lose your chance for a quick sale because of poor curb appeal.

Four Steps to Great Curb Appeal

"An appealing 'curb-scape' is like a living welcome mat, inviting potential buyers to linger and take a closer look. A well-maintained yard with a fresh appearance speaks volumes. Include your outdoor entrance in your home staging and your time and energy will be rewarded."

Norma McKercher, home stager and avid gardener

When staging the exterior of your house, follow the same four-step process used to stage the interior: de-cluttering/depersonalizing, repairing and upgrading, cleaning, and styling.

Begin by assessing your house's exterior as objectively as possible. Stand across the street and imagine that you are seeing it for the first time. Maybe take photos of your house and see how it looks through a camera's lens. Does the paint or siding look fresh and attractive? Does your house fit in nicely with the style and colour of the neighbours' houses? Is the yard neat or are toys and other items strewn about? Do overgrown trees or shrubs obscure the front of the house? Are the windows clean and the roof and gutters in good condition? Is the house number easily visible?

Next, walk up to the front door using the path that buyers will take. Is the walkway even and clear or is it cracked and weedy? Is the front entrance welcoming or are visitors greeted with cobwebs? Is the front door in excellent condition or is it scuffed, peeling, or weathered?

Set Priorities Before You Begin Staging

Set priorities and make a plan before you begin. Focus your efforts on improving areas that are most likely to make a bad impression. For example, from the street view, do your gutters look clear (even though you may know they are due for a cleaning) or can you actually see debris spilling over or small saplings growing from them? Are they neatly attached and reasonably straight, or are they noticeably sagging and bending? Leaving these in extremely poor condition sends a bad message. However, don't waste your time and efforts cleaning gutters that already appear fine.

Beginning with the most glaring issues, then, do as much as you reasonably can within your time frame and budget. Once you're done with these areas, and if you have the time, you can then stage the other exterior areas. Although your "wish list" of staging tasks may seem long, doing as much as you can is what will make your house show better than the vast majority of the others. Buyers will notice.

Also focus on the areas that buyers see first; usually this is the front yard and front of the house, but your house may be different so consider where buyers are most likely to first set their eyes. For example, if you expect that buyers will park at the side of the house and walk around to the front, take care of that side of the house as well as its front. Will they be able to view some of the back yard before they move to the front door? If so, deal with the specific part of the back yard that they'll see as they walk up.

Step 1: De-clutter and Depersonalize

The yard and front of the house can easily look cluttered if there are too many items competing for attention or blocking a clear view of the house.

Just as you did inside the house, remove items from the outside of the house that are highly personal, taste-specific, or don't absolutely need to be there, such as the following:

- **Bikes and toys**. Put bikes away in the garage or shed or move them out of sight. Remove all rarely used play equipment—like a play structure, sandbox, basketball hoop, hockey nets, or a skateboard ramp—to make the yard seem larger and neater. However, if you think that young families will be looking at the house, consider leaving a play structure in place in the backyard to show that there is plenty of room for a play area. (However, always remove play structures from the front yard.)

- **Gardening tools**. Remove all evidence of the work involved in keeping your yard maintained. Store lawnmower, rakes, empty flowerpots, watering cans, and other equipment out of sight. If you must leave a garden hose out, coil it neatly (preferably on a hose reel) and set it at the side of the house.

- **Lawn ornaments**. Although items like statues, gazing balls, wind spinners, and garden gnomes add character and whimsy, remove them when listing your home. Like wallpaper inside the house, these are very taste specific and many people will not appreciate them. They also attract attention, thus distracting the buyer's focus away from the house and yard.

- **Decorations on the house.** Pack away anything on the house that is taste-specific or personalized such as wind chimes, flags, banners, dried wreaths, name plaques, or other signs at the front door. Also take down out-of-season Christmas lights and decorations. Lights are appropriate between late November and early January, but even then, limit your display to simple light strings.

- **Too many pots and hanging plants.** Although containers of plants and flowers help to beautify the front yard, too many make the yard look cluttered. Keep containers and hanging plants to a minimum; if the front steps are small, one container or hanging plant is plenty. If the front steps are large, one container on each side of the door looks great.

- **Garbage cans, recycling bins**. Unless it's a pick-up day, keep your garbage possible and recycling bins out of view, if possible. If they must be stored on the driveway, place them as far to the side of the house as possible, and move them reasonably soon after pick up.

- **An RV or trailer parked in the driveway or on the street in front of the house**. Unless you have dedicated RV parking, move your trailer or RV to storage until you sell the house. It will likely obstruct the view of the house and make the yard look cluttered. The same applies to unused parked cars.

- **Scrap piles**. Some people store scraps of wood, left-over building materials, and other odds and ends in a pile in the yard. Even if it can't be readily seen at first glance, it's a good idea to get rid of a scrap pile. If you have a lot of junk to remove, consider renting a dumpster or hiring a junk removal service.

- **Dead plants and trees.** Removing dead or dying plants and trees will make the whole yard look much better. Removing a large tree and its stump can be a big job and can also be dangerous, so consider hiring a professional.

- **Overgrown or woody shrubs**. Trim or remove shrubs or trees that block a window or path (even if only partially) or obscure a good view of the house.

Step 2: Repairs and Upgrades

Make sure potential buyers don't see problems as they drive by or walk up to your doorstep. Take care of all needed repairs and updates outside the house or you risk scaring off potential buyers before they even set foot in the door.

Repairs

Keep up with regular maintenance and attend to even seemingly minor repairs, including the following:

- Repair large cracks, leaks, or signs of moisture on foundation walls.
- Repair cracks and uneven surfaces, sinking bricks, or crumbling concrete on driveways and walkways. Remove oil stains on driveways. Gravel driveways may need to be graded. Asphalt driveways may need to be resealed.
- Ensure front steps are in good repair. Replace broken steps or handrails.
- Re-seed bald spots in lawn. Consider re-sodding if the lawn is in desperate condition.
- Remove moss and weeds from walkways.
- Prune deadwood from trees and shrubs.
- Clean gutters and downspouts and ensure they are securely attached to the house; replace damaged downspouts. Paint over rust or streaks on downspouts.
- From the ground, check the roof for curling shingles or sagging sections. Contact a professional for possible repair or replacement.
- Ensure the doorbell works and is in good condition. You'd be surprised by how many listings have doorbells that are broken or held together with duct tape.
- Replace damaged vinyl siding, or repair damaged stucco.
- Sand and repaint blistered or peeling paint on the siding, trim, shutters, and garage door.
- Ensure fences and gates are in good repair. Paint or stain the fence if needed.

- Repair or remove the exterior screen door if it is in poor condition. Consider removing it even if it is in good condition in order to give buyers a good view of the front door.
- Ensure all light bulbs are working so that buyers will be able to see your house if they drive by in the evening. Install the highest wattage bulb recommended for the fixture.
- Repair or stain decking or porches, as needed.
- Paint over any graffiti on your fence, garage, or shed.

Upgrades

For exterior upgrades, focus on what potential buyers will notice first: the house colour and front entry.

House Colour. If your house is painted an appealing colour, it may only require minor touch-ups, usually to the trim but wherever else it may be peeling or blistered. However, consider repainting if your house is a bold or unusual colour, the paint is in very poor condition and looks shabby, or the current colour generally doesn't blend in well with neighbouring houses. Although repainting is a big job, if it's absolutely necessary it will be well worth the time and money. The colour and condition of the paint (or of the siding or stucco) makes a tremendous impact on overall curb appeal.

Many designers suggest choosing a paint scheme consisting of three colours: a main colour for the siding, a complementary colour for the trim, and an accent colour for the door. For the main colour, choose a stylish and neutral colour that complements fixed elements such as the roof, brick, or stonework. It should also blend in well with the surroundings.

Some designers also recommend that the exterior colour of the house reflect the predominant colour scheme used inside the house.

For inspiration, check out paint manufacturers' websites (such as benjaminmoore.com or para.com) to see trends in exterior house and trim colours and ways to combine these colours. Many sites have software that enable you to import a picture of your house and try various colours on it for a quick preview of what it would look like. Also pay attention to the colours used on new homes in your city. Builders usually follow current trends, so if you think these colours would blend nicely into your neighborhood, go ahead and copy what you like.

Because exterior paint colour makes such a dramatic impact, it's always a good idea to consult with a professional home stager or a decorator at a paint store before making a final decision.

Front Door. The front door is the focal point of the house and a place where buyers are sure to linger before stepping inside. Even if you don't repaint the house, consider painting the front door a bold, glossy colour to really grab attention. Choose a colour that makes the door stand out but still complements the house colour, such as a chocolate brown door for a cream-coloured house or a black or red door for a beige house. Box 7-1 includes some of our favorite colour selections for an eye-catching front door.

Box 7.1 Recommended Front Door Colours, PARA Paints

Blues	Greens	Reds	Browns
Huronia P2115-03	Papineau Tint 3 P2078-02	She Loves Pink P5085-73	Bateau Brown P2072-03
Lefroy Glacier P2701-02	Mountain Dew P5113-73	Rich Bordeaux P5087-73	Black Creek P2074-05
Starless Sky P5155-62	Core Strength P5171-85D	Asian Rose P5077-85	Coffee Beans P5239-62D

Although a fresh coat of paint can do wonders, replace the door if it is in very poor condition. Remove old or mismatched screen doors to better show off your front door, and polish the hardware (or replace, if necessary) to make it shine.

Don't forget about the garage door. Make sure its paint is in good condition. If you need to repaint it, apply the same or similar colour that is used on the rest of the house. Unlike the front door, the garage door should blend in with the house.

Lights, Mailbox, and House Numbers. Other simple upgrades to the front entry include updating light fixtures, the mailbox, and the house numbers.

If the exterior light fixture is damaged or very outdated, consider installing a new fixture. Contemporary outdoor lighting fixtures can instantly add life to a tired exterior. If you are installing just one fixture beside the front door, place it on the side near the doorknob about one-third of the way down from the top of the door. If you're installing two fixtures on either side of the door, place them a little higher, about one-quarter of the way down from the top of the door.

House numbers need to be easily seen from the road so buyers can find you. If they aren't, replace them with a new style that's more visible or spray paint them to contrast with your siding. If your house is situated back from the road, use an address stake at the end of the driveway.

Many homeowners overlook the mailbox, but all too often mailboxes are dingy, beaten up, too small, or don't close properly. The mailbox must be clean and in excellent condition because buyers usually look at it while they are waiting to be let in. A good cleaning and polishing may be all that's needed to freshen it up. If this doesn't help, spray paint it black or replace it with a new mailbox. Choose a classic design that's in scale with the size of your front entry.

Good online retail sites that sell mailboxes and house numbers and ship to Canada include Chiasso.com, Housenumbertiles.com, and 360yardware.com.

Step 3: Cleaning

Once you're done repairs and upgrades, it's time to clean the exterior of the house. If you haven't repainted the house, it will definitely benefit from a thorough cleaning.

Begin by removing dirt and cobwebs from the corners and siding, concentrating on the front entry area. Clean the ceiling of the porch and the overhang over the front door. Use a power washer to remove the webs, or you can try using a shop vac to vacuum them.

Painted walls or vinyl siding can be power-washed for a renewed look. Whether you hire a professional or do it yourself, check first to make sure that the power spray isn't so strong that it will damage the wall. Keep the nozzle three to four feet away from the surface and don't spray for too long at any one point. Spray from top to bottom so the dirty water runs down.

To clean stucco or brick walls, apply a solution of 1 gallon of warm water, 1 quart bleach, and 1 cup trisodium phosphate (TSP). Lightly scrub with a soft bristle brush and then rinse thoroughly with clean water. Test the solution on a small, inconspicuous area first to ensure it won't damage the surface. You could also try a commercial cleaning product for stucco, such as CLR, Quikrete Concrete, or Stucco Wash.

Remember, you don't have to spot clean the siding over the entire house; simply focus on cleaning the front entry and areas that the buyers will see as they walk up to the door.

Other areas that need cleaning include the front door (if it hasn't been freshly painted), doorknob, exterior windows, and light fixtures, especially those by the front door. Empty dead bugs or moths from the fixture and wash thoroughly with soapy water. Chapter 5 gives details on cleaning windows. Remember to clean the dirt off the windowsills.

Cleaning for curb appeal also includes tending to your yard. Sweep the driveway and sidewalks to make a safe, neat, and welcoming path to the house. Remove all debris, including leaves and grass clippings. In winter, promptly shovel and sand all pathways whenever needed. Also sand icy spots around downspouts to ensure visitors won't slip.

In the spring and summer, weed and fertilize the flowerbeds and lawn regularly. Of course, mow and water the lawn frequently so that the grass looks lush.

Step 4: Styling

Although the exterior of the house and the yard don't require accessories, there are other ways to add style here:

- Purchase a new mat for the front door that coordinates with the house colours and extends the full width of the door.

- Take a look at your landscaping. Are there any bare spots near the house where a new shrub or flowers could go to add some interest and colour?

- Choose annuals or perennials with colours that complement the house and surroundings.

- Succulents are very popular with their myriad of shapes, sizes, textures, and colours, and they make a dynamic statement.

- Make sure not to crowd plants too near a pathway or doorway.

- Landscaping can be as simple as placing two large containers of single-coloured annuals by the front door, one on either side. If your entry way is small, use just one large container. Ask for help at your local green house in selecting appropriate plants for a lush presentation. (Remember to consistently water and deadhead.)

- Add fresh mulch to your flowerbeds and around trees. Choose a natural brown colour; avoid red mulch. As well as helping the soil retain moisture, mulch makes a yard look neat and well tended. If you already have enough mulch, gently rake it to refresh it.

- Edge the lawn. Make defined borders around sidewalks, flowerbeds, and driveways.

- Be careful with hanging pots of annuals. Too many pots can quickly make the house look cluttered. Instead, opt for fewer, larger pots or none at all.

- In the winter, create a seasonal arrangement in a planter at the front door using red dogwood branches and live seasonal greens. Artificial berries can be added for colour.

- If you have a pool, ensure that the water is crystal clear. If you want to make a vignette, set out some patio furniture, a few beach towels, and a tray with tall plastic drinking glasses.

- On a front porch, arrange two outdoor chairs and a small table to create a conversation area. Consider placing a mason jar of flowers or a book and pitcher of iced tea on the table to create a vignette.

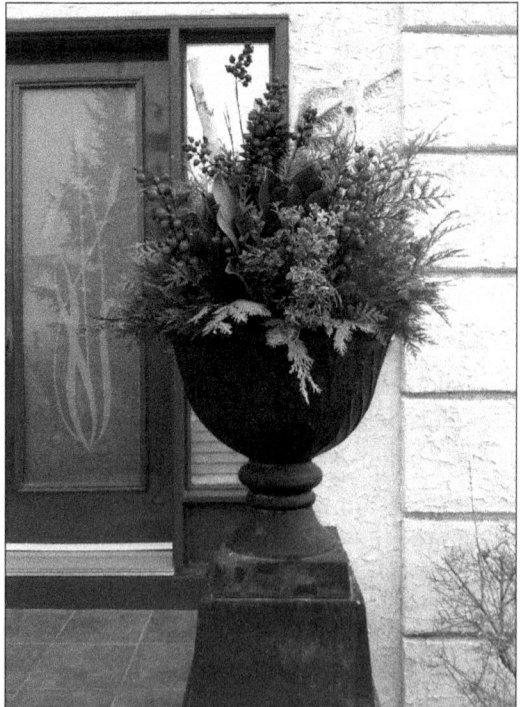

A winter planter arrangement featuring birch branches, evergreen boughs, and red berries provides a warm welcome at this front door.

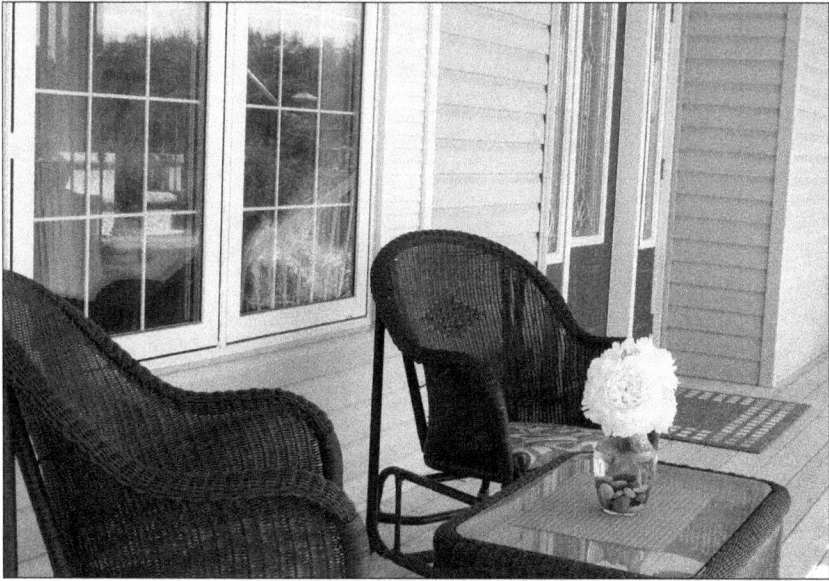

This cozy scene on the front porch invites potential buyers to come on in.

- Take a look at the view in the windows from the outside. Make sure draperies or blinds inside the house are hanging neatly and evenly so they look good from the outside. Especially at the front windows, make sure the view inside is a good one.

Once you're done staging the exterior, keep it in good condition at all times. You never know when potential buyers might drive by to check out the house and neighbourhood.

This house already has nice curb appeal with a neutral colour, nice trim, attractive mailbox and house number, and an eye-catching front door. However, there's room for improvement. How many problems can you spot?

With the clutter stored, the blinds straightened, and the wind chime and name plaque removed, all this house needed was a touch of colour from flowers and a nice bench to make its curb appeal even better.

Curb Appeal CHECKLIST

Declutter/Depersonalize
- ☐ Put away bikes, toys, gardening tools and hoses, play structures, and any other items left out in the yard.
- ☐ Remove lawn ornaments such as statues, gazing balls, windspinners, and garden gnomes.
- ☐ Remove personalized items hanging in the front entrance, such as name plaques, wind chimes, flags, and banners.
- ☐ Take down out-of-season Christmas lights and decorations.
- ☐ Store garbage cans and recycling bins out of sight or out of the way.
- ☐ Move RVs, trailers, and unused cars to storage.
- ☐ Remove scrap piles.
- ☐ Remove dead plants and trees.
- ☐ Trim or remove shrubs or trees that block a window or path or obscure the view of the house.
- ☐ Remove exterior screen doors so buyers have a good view of the front door.

Repairs
- ☐ Ensure foundation walls are free of large cracks, leaks, or signs of moisture.
- ☐ Repair cracks and uneven surfaces, sinking bricks, or crumbling concrete in driveway and walkways.
- ☐ Remove moss and weeds from walkways.
- ☐ Grade gravel driveway, if needed; re-seal asphalt driveway, if needed.
- ☐ Remove oil stains from driveway.
- ☐ Replace broken risers or handrails at front step.
- ☐ Re-seed bald spots in lawn.
- ☐ Prune trees and shrubs.

- ❑ Clean gutters and downspouts, and ensure they are securely attached to the house; replace damaged downspouts, and paint over rust or streaks.
- ❑ From the ground, check the roof for curling shingles or sagging sections. Contact a professional for repair or replacement.
- ❑ Replace damaged vinyl siding.
- ❑ Repair damaged stucco.
- ❑ Replace old caulking.
- ❑ Sand and repaint blistered or peeling paint, including on trim, shutters, and garage door.
- ❑ Repair or stain decking or porches, as needed.
- ❑ Ensure fences are in good repair and graffiti-free. Paint or stain if needed.
- ❑ Replace burned-out light bulbs. Use the highest wattage recommended for the fixture.
- ❑ Ensure the doorbell works and doorknocker is in good repair.

Upgrades

- ❑ Repaint exterior of the house if the paint is in poor condition (faded, cracked, or peeling), is a bold or unusual colour, or doesn't blend in well with the neighbouring houses.
- ❑ Paint the front door a bold, eye-catching colour that complements the house colour.
- ❑ Paint the garage door a colour that blends in with the house colour.
- ❑ Replace broken or outdated light fixtures.
- ❑ Paint or replace the mailbox.
- ❑ Paint or replace house numbers.

Clean

- ❑ Remove dirt and cobwebs from the porch and around the front door.
- ❑ Power wash vinyl siding or painted walls.

- Scrub stucco or brick walls.
- Clean windows and doors, including the hardware on doors.
- Wash the light fixtures.
- Sweep or shovel the driveway and sidewalks.
- Sand all icy spots.
- Clean gutters and downspouts.
- Mow, fertilize, and water the lawn.
- Weed the flowerbeds.

Style

- Place a new mat at the front door.
- Fill bare spots in the landscaping with a new shrub or plant.
- Add fresh mulch on flowerbeds and around trees, or rake existing mulch to refresh it.
- Water, mow, and edge the lawn routinely.
- Place a large planter or two by the front door and fill with annuals in the summer or evergreens in the winter.
- Arrange a welcoming seating area in the front porch.
- Make sure draperies or blinds are hanging neatly.

chapter eight

Special Considerations

THE GENERAL STAGING PRINCIPLES and steps presented so far can be applied to almost all homes and situations. However, some special circumstances require slightly different approaches.

This chapter addresses special staging considerations, including:

- Staging a vacant house
- Staging in different seasons
- Staging tips for various life stages
- When you have to get your house on the market fast

Staging a Vacant House

"Staging a vacant house is a great investment. A few simple staging tricks make the house more 'homey,' helping buyers to imagine what it would be like to live there and form a connection with the home. It's a marketing tool that we've used for years to sell our properties quickly. Staging definitely works!"

Brenda W. Couros, K. Ash & Co. Development Corp.

Sometimes homeowners have no choice but to move before their house is sold. Usually they take all their belongings and leave the house completely empty, or sometimes they leave stacks of boxes behind, intending to move them once the house is sold. Usually they lower the heat and close all the curtains, and sometimes they even shut off the utilities to save on expenses. Vacant homes like these, and even empty new homes that have never been lived in, consistently prove to be difficult to sell. Vacant homes are reported to sit on the market 50% to 70% longer and sell for 5% to 6% less than occupied homes.

Vacant homes are more difficult to sell because buyers have difficulty forming an emotional connection with them. Empty homes are bare and impersonal. Without furniture to show the purpose of a room or accessories to add colour and personality, they are less likely to draw buyers in or be memorable. As a result, buyers feel less emotionally connected to these homes and less likely to imagine living there.

Also, with nothing to make them slow down during their tour and without even a chair to sit on, buyers are less likely to linger in a vacant home. In fact, potential buyers generally breeze through a vacant home in as little as five minutes, whereas they'll stay for as long as 40 minutes in a furnished home. The less time spent in a house, the less they'll remember about it and the less likely they'll be to make an offer.

This bedroom has a fresh, neutral paint colour, two closets, and a lovely chandelier—yet it looks bare and uninviting.

With some basic furnishings, fabric, and a nice mirror, this bedroom is much warmer and more memorable.

Vacant homes can also signal that the seller is desperate, especially when basic yard care is neglected. Flyers piled up in the mailbox, leaves strewn about the walkway, and a weedy and overgrown lawn and flower-bed make the house look abandoned. As a result, buyers interested in a vacant house tend to make low-ball offers.

Staging a vacant house, therefore, is essential for a quick and profitable sale.

Maintaining a Vacant House

The first priority when staging a vacant home is to make sure that it doesn't look abandoned, especially from the outside. Keep the exterior in top shape by asking a friend or neighbour to help maintain it. If you can't find dependable volunteers, hire a yard service or a property management company. Keeping a vacant property maintained is so important that any money spent on this will be a good investment.

At least weekly, have someone:

- Pick up flyers and mail from the mailbox.
- Remove cobwebs from the front entryway.
- Mow and water the lawn.
- Weed and water the flowerbeds.
- Sweep or shovel the entryway, walkways, and driveway.
- Rake leaves in the fall.

Similarly, make sure the interior of the home is maintained. Have someone, paid or volunteer, check inside the house at least weekly and look for signs of leaks, ensure the furnace or air conditioning is working, dust the main living areas, and ventilate the house by opening the windows and turning on fans while they're there.

You can help by making a few arrangements before you leave:

- Keep utilities on, which allows the real estate agent to turn on the lights when showing the home and also enables the home inspector to do a thorough job.
- Set the furnace or air conditioner to a pleasant temperature. In the winter, set the furnace to about 20°C (68°F); if you have a programmable thermostat, lower the temperature at night to save on heating cost. In summer, set the air conditioner to about 23°C (73°F). Consider

leaving ceiling fans on to circulate the air and decrease staleness.

- Install timers to automatically turn on few interior and exterior lights in the evenings. Consider installing solar-powered lights along the pathway leading to the door to add more lighting without adding to your electrical bill.

Check Your Insurance

Check whether your homeowner's policy covers your home while it is vacant; some policies do not cover vacant homes due to increased risk of damage should a fire or other disaster occur while vacant. If your policy does cover vacant homes, find out whether it stipulates how often the property must be checked.

Styling a Vacant House

Surprisingly, a room often appears smaller without furnishings. Without furniture to give perspective, buyers often have difficulty getting a good sense of the size, or even the purpose, of the rooms. Even worse, every little flaw in an empty room—such as nail holes, dingy ceilings, or scratched floors—appears that much more noticeable because there's nothing else for buyers to look at.

Although the house doesn't have to look as if it's is occupied, leaving behind a few pieces of furniture, art, and accessories helps to present your house at its best. Furniture not only makes the room more appealing, it also demonstrates how the space can be used. If you can, use your own furnishings, borrow some from friends or family, or rent some from a home staging company.

It isn't necessary to stage every vacant room. Key areas to stage include the kitchen, dining area, living room, master bedroom, and ensuite. Use just a few pieces to highlight the best features of these rooms. Below are suggestions for staging each critical area of your home. Depending on the size of the rooms, you may need to add or subtract from this list.

Kitchen. Add an artificial plant by the sink or window, a large bowl of artificial green apples or pears on the counter or island, and two bar stools at the island. On the counter, display some nice stemware on a tray or an attractive teapot with two matching cups.

Dining Area. Leave a small table with two to four chairs. Add a centerpiece of nice silk flowers or a cluster of interesting vases. Set the table with a placemat at each setting, a dinner plate with a salad plate on top of it, and a glass. Consider laying a large area rug under the table if the floor is tile, cork, hardwood or laminate. For a final touch, include a large picture on the wall directly opposite the entrance to the room.

Staged with rented furniture, the dining room in this vacant house looks very appealing.

Living Room. The furnishings in a vacant living room can be as simple as one chair, an end table, and a lamp arranged to showcase the focal point. If you're able to do more, the room can be improved with an area rug, a sofa, two chairs (or a loveseat), a coffee table, and end tables. To accessorize, include a large artificial plant in the corner, hang a large picture above the sofa or fireplace, and place a lamp on one of the end tables. Include a bulb in the lamp and plug it in so the real estate agent can turn it on for showings. Also include a few decorative items (such as candles or a bowl) for the coffee table and the other end table.

Master Bedroom. Stage a master bedroom with a queen bed made up with neutral bedding and coordinating throw and toss cushions. If necessary, you could use an inflatable camping bed that sets up on legs and then cover it with bedding and cushions like a normal bed. Add two bed-side tables, a lamp for one of the tables, and a large picture above the bed.

Ensuite. Keep the ensuite simple with just a nice soap dispenser and an artificial plant on the counter top. Leave two new white or neutral-coloured towels (use the hotel fold and hang them over the towel rack or stack them on the counter). Finally, hang a picture (about 12" x 12") over the toilet, about 16" from the top of the tank.

The bathroom in this vacant house is nice but boring.

With the addition of only three accessories, the bathroom is now interesting and cheerful.

Staging for the Seasons

Houses are bought and sold during all seasons of the year. If you live in a climate with distinct seasons, a few special staging considerations are needed for each season.

Spring

- Be extra cautious about spring runoff. Make sure to shovel snow away from the foundation of your house before it starts to melt. Dig snow out of window wells.
- Get your flowerbeds started as soon as possible.
- If you have a dog, clean up your yard as soon as possible and re-seed bare patches in the lawn.
- Set up your outdoor furniture, even if it's not quite warm enough for it.
- Hose down your vinyl siding.
- Double check for bug or mouse infestations. Hire an exterminator if necessary.
- Introduce cheerful, light spring colours in your accessories, such as pale green, light blue, and white.
- Include arrangements of spring flowers in the house, such as tulips, even if there's still snow on the ground. Seeing early signs of spring will put buyers in a good mood.

Summer

- Maintain your flowers throughout the summer—consistently water, weed, deadhead, and fertilize to keep them looking fresh all summer.
- If you have space at your front door or porch, include a rocking chair or bench with pretty cushions to welcome your buyers.
- Keep your mailbox and light fixtures near the front door clear of dust and cobwebs.
- Water and mow your lawn frequently. Keep weeds under control.
- Sweep walkways as needed.
- Set up a hammock in the back yard to show that it is perfect for relaxation.

- Ensure that your home is a comfortable temperature for showings. If you don't have air conditioning, keep the house cool by closing drapes and blinds to prevent sunshine from heating your home. (But open them for showings.) Turn on ceiling fans if you have them, and open windows at night to cool the house.
- Leave lemonade or bottled water in an ice bucket on the kitchen table for buyers if you are without air conditioning.
- Consider planning a vacation during the time your home is listed. As long as you are accessible to your real estate agent by phone and fax, it might be easier to be away from your home.

Fall

- Make sure you have enough indoor lighting to brighten up the house as the days get shorter.
- Take care of fall yard cleanup chores as soon as possible.
- Make your home cozier by adding a throw blanket in the living room or setting out fall candles.
- Don't go overboard with Thanksgiving or Halloween decorations. (Forgo the fake cobwebs for this year.)

Winter

- Shovel your driveway and walkways, even if there's just a dusting of snow. Ensure that all walkways are clear of ice.
- If you will be listing your home over the holidays, keep decorations very simple. For example, add fresh evergreen boughs on the mantel and display seasonal candles on the table. Don't clutter every surface with decorations.
- If you have a Christmas tree, make sure you still have good traffic flow throughout the room. Remove some pieces of furniture, if necessary, or set up a small tree this year to avoid making the room too cramped.
- Avoid placing decorations on your lawn, front door, or the areas of the home that can be viewed when you first step into the house.
- Remove Christmas lights as soon as possible after early January.
- Make sure your home is comfortably warm when people come to view it.

- Wipe away condensation that may form on the inside of your windows on very cold days. It helps to keep blinds raised a little to allow better airflow and prevent condensation buildup.
- Ensure that all boots and jackets are put away in the closet. Winter jackets, mittens, hats, snow pants, etc., should not be visible when entering the home. If you don't have a front closet, avoid hanging coats on hooks along the wall. Instead, use another area of the house to store your outerwear during showings.
- Ensure that you have a large mat at the front door. People will feel uncomfortable if they have to struggle to stay on the mat when entering and won't want to step on your flooring with their boots.
- Make sure every light bulb works, both inside and outside the house. You'll need lots of light for winter showings.
- Use throws on chairs and sofas to create a sense of warmth.
- If you have a gas fireplace, turn it on in for showings to add warmth and a feeling of coziness.
- Try to schedule showings during the daytime to make use of as much natural light as possible. Open all blinds and window coverings.
- During open houses, consider having warm cider or coffee available (leave a stack of insulated paper cups).

Home Staging for Various Life Stages

Depending on your phase of life, you may need to focus your staging efforts a little differently. While these are generalizations, they tend to be true of many staging clients. Sellers have different staging needs depending on whether they are moving from their first homes, moving a family to a larger home, or selling a home in retirement.

Selling Your Starter Home

Homeowners selling their first house to move into a larger one may be in a situation where they have furnished their home with hand-me-downs. Is your home rather sparsely furnished with a mix of items? Is your décor saying, "university days" or "retrieved from my parents' basement?"

Maybe you have pieced together the décor as you saved to move to a different area or a larger home.

If this is your situation, you may benefit from paying particular attention to how you style your home. Your décor does have an impact on buyers, even if it is not being sold with the home. Hence, furnishings, accessories, and artwork that coordinate and fit nicely into the space will make a good impression and help showcase your home.

You don't need luxurious items to stage your starter home. Most likely, the people interested in buying your house will be young, first-time buyers. Consider what their needs and expectations will be. Usually they would not be swayed by high-end furnishings or décor, but rather would be looking for a functional, tasteful, and practical home at a fair price.

If you are certain about what new items you would like for your next home, consider purchasing some now to help stage your house. For example, if you know you want a brown leather sofa for your next home, buying it now and getting rid of Grandma's old floral sofa may be well worth it. If you prefer to wait to make new furniture purchases, consider borrowing or renting living room furniture. Larger cities have furniture rental stores where you can rent furniture and accessories for most rooms in your home.

It may be difficult to think about spending when money is tight and you are eager to make a nice profit on your home. If you are determined to wait on furniture purchases, some other minor purchases are likely to pay off. A new mat at the front door, fresh bath towels, up-to-date toss cushions, neutral drapery panels, inexpensively framed photos or art, and new lamps are definitely worth considering.

When marketing a home to first-time buyers, any upgrades you can offer will help you to outshine the competition. A new countertop, fresh flooring, a small deck, or a well-landscaped yard is especially appealing to property virgins.

Selling a Family Home

Helping your Kids Adjust. If you have children in the house, you will have certain challenges to address when staging your house.

The first challenge is to be sensitive to the children's feelings during the staging process. Many children don't like change, and moving can arouse strong emotions in them, including fear and anxiety. Very young children may not understand why their belongings are being packed away or why the house looks and feels so different after staging. Older children may dread leaving their friends, school, and familiar surroundings.

Keep the lines of communication open during the staging process. Talking about issues and their thoughts and feelings is the most important way to help children deal with the stresses of moving and home staging. Stay positive about the move by focusing on the good things to look forward to in the new house.

Try to explain to young children why you are staging the house, keeping your explanations clear and simple. For example, say, "We're packing away some of your toys now but we're not throwing them out. We're just setting them aside where they'll be safe, and they'll be waiting for you at the new house." Or, "We need to move the furniture around so that people will want to buy this house." Some children feel better when they can see the packed boxes before they are sealed.

Involving kids in the planning and work of staging their rooms helps them feel more in control of the process. Being invited to participate is better than feeling like the changes are being forced on them. Ask the children to help label their boxes. Some may enjoy decorating their boxes with markers, stickers, or crayons. Help younger children write their name on their boxes.

For older children and teens, staging their rooms can become complicated if they don't want to cooperate. Be respectful of their feelings and concerns. Teens can have difficulty letting go of familiar surroundings and possessions and may strongly resist the needed changes. Patience, empathy, and good communication are your best response. Assure them that in the new house they'll be able to arrange their rooms in their own style. Address any underlying fears or anxieties about the move. Review the tips in Chapter 2 for ideas on helping older children say good-bye to their home.

Staging Considerations for a Family Home. Once the kids are onboard, you can turn your attention to staging. If you expect that potential buyers will mainly be families, stage the house with family needs in mind.

When staging a family home, it's not necessary to hide the fact that you have kids. Show that kids live there, but reduce the clutter that usually comes with them. De-cluttering and depersonalizing, therefore, is very important to highlight the storage space and living space that families want.

If you're using a spare bedroom for another purpose, such as a sewing room, change it back to a bedroom. If you have an extra bathroom in the basement, spruce it up to make it as appealing as a main floor bathroom. For example, for visual interest, add a silk fern, a tray of seashells, or tall glass vase of wicker balls.

Create as much storage space as possible by packing and storing excess items from all closets, cupboards, and storage areas. Work hard to clean up your basement and garage.

Most families with children have a lot of toys, DVDs, and gaming systems. Pack as many as you can now to free up space. This is your chance to donate all those toys and games that the children have outgrown or no longer use. Store toys neatly in bins, boxes, or baskets. Tidy video game areas by providing storage bins for the games and controllers. Ideally, store toys in the children's rooms and in one dedicated play area. "Toy-free" zones include the living room, dining room, kitchen (highchair and booster seats are acceptable), bathrooms, master bedroom, and office/den.

In the kids' rooms, remove all posters, stickers on the walls and door, items that display the child's name, and toys with many small pieces. Keep only the best quality toys to display (let go of the Happy Meal trinkets).

Safety First

Buyers with children will pay particular attention to whether your home is safe for kids. Attending to repairs that represent tripping or falling hazards is especially important. If you have a pool, a fence around it is required by code.

Stage children's rooms by focusing on a colour theme for accessories and then displaying books and toys that match this theme. For example, shelves in a kid's room can be staged using hardcover books, small toys, and stuffed animals in colours that coordinate with the bedding and paint in the room.

When styling these shelves in a little boy's room, the stager decided to display books and accessories to coordinate with the blue and green colour scheme throughout the room.

Place a small grouping of stuffies in coordinating colours on the bed. Strive for a neat, organized, airy feel. Build in as much cuteness as you possibly can. For example, display a tea party for three stuffed animals around a small table. Hang a fun or whimsical piece of art on the wall. Or create a vignette of a Playmobil scene or a puzzle in progress on a small rug or table.

When you stage the backyard, highlight its usefulness as a safe play area for children. Make sure the fence is in good repair and the lawn is lush and inviting. If you have a play structure that's in good condition, leave it set up in a corner of the yard.

Selling a Home to Downsize

For some, unfortunate circumstances such as a job loss or divorce means downsizing to a more affordable property. Regardless of your reasons for needing a smaller home, staging a larger home with plans to move to a smaller one can be tricky.

If money is tight, investing your own time and energy into de-cluttering and cleaning will be particularly important. Even if you do nothing else, a clean and organized house is significantly more saleable.

De-cluttering is absolutely free, and not only will it help to sell your house, it will also make it easier for you to move into a smaller home. Eliminate from your home anything that you don't love, need, or use. You may need to scale back on furniture for your next home, so sell or give away the pieces that you won't need later. Be careful, however, to leave enough in your current home to help it show well. Consider selling the pieces you won't be taking with you (e.g., a large dining room table) and borrowing or renting items to replace them.

If you can, leave ample time for sorting through your belongings and selling or giving away the things you no longer need. Think carefully about what pieces will be the most useful and fit best into your next home. Favor a small chest of drawers over a long, large dresser. Find a new home for your sectional, and plan on taking your sofa or loveseat instead.

If there is nothing in the budget for repairs or styling, do what you can. Be creative. Stain on an armchair? Strategically place a toss cushion or throw to hide the damage. No money to replace a pink toilet and sink? Play it up with a bouquet of fresh, bright pink flowers on the vanity.

Selling an Older Home after Many Years In It

After people have lived in their house for decades, selling it for top dollar can sometimes be a challenge. Homeowners who are in the same place for a long period of time sometimes stop updating decorative details. A home that isn't current—even if it has been well maintained—isn't what most people are seeking. Buyers know that outdated homes require a lot of time, energy, and money to make the changes they'd want.

If you are helping older relatives prepare their home for sale, or if you yourself are selling your home after many years in it, your best strategy is to focus on de-cluttering and cleaning. Packing away family photos, collections, and keepsakes that make the home very personal is a necessary step. Remove handmade items such as embroidered cushions, tablecloths, and crocheted throws. Remove some furniture if the room feels stuffed.

Think carefully about any updating you do in order to sell the house. If the entire house is outdated, the cost of redoing everything may not be recouped by the sale. Choosing to update one part of the house but not all of it may have limited success. Replacing the linoleum flooring in the kitchen, for example, won't have the same impact if the rest of the kitchen is circa 1970. An entirely outdated home should likely be left as is and priced accordingly. Discuss the issue with your real estate agent.

You can still improve your chances for a quicker sale, however, by taking care of all basic repairs, removing wallpaper, and repainting walls in a popular, neutral colour.

When styling the house, do what you can to update the look without breaking the bank. Focus on basic accessories that can help to make it look more current: lighting, window coverings, hardware, and accessories. Replace outdated lamps and light fixtures with new simple yet stylish ones. Take down heavy and outdated curtains and valences to update the look and let in more light. If privacy is an issue, invest in some new blinds. Replace cabinet knobs for a simple, quick update. Buy, borrow, or rent a few accessories to add a punch of colour and interest in the room (see Chapter 6 for details on accessorizing).

To give your listing an edge in the market, highlight features of your house that newer homes in your community may not have. Chances are your yard and neighbourhood have mature trees. This is a definite plus. Set a café table and two chairs under a large tree to highlight a mature yard. Set a porch swing at the back of a generously sized lot to draw attention to a spacious backyard. If you have original hardwood floors in good condition, remove area rugs to show as much floor as possible, as long as the sunlight hasn't faded the hardwood. Older homes sometimes have larger bedrooms. If you have extra bedrooms and you think young families will be interested in the house, style these rooms as children's rooms, showcasing their spaciousness.

Staging in a Hurry

If you're listing your house right away and only have time to read one section of this book, this is it. If you don't have much time (or energy, or interest, or help) to prepare your home, it's especially important to be strategic. Make the most from your effort by focusing on what matters most.

- **Focus on what people will immediately see when they approach your house.** Work from the front yard, to the front door, and then toward the back of your house. The basement will likely be viewed after the main floor, so work on this area only after you have completed a quick stage on the main floor.

- **In your front yard, shovel, sweep, mow, and trim back shrubs near the doorway.** Put your garbage can out of view and park vehicles away from the front of your home before showings. Put bikes and toys away, and stack lawn furniture out of view from doorway or windows of the house.

- **Inside the house, make your primary goals to quickly de-clutter it and hide personal items.** Aim for a clean, spacious look. Don't worry about packing and organizing. Move through the rooms with a large bag and collect papers and magazines for recycling. Have another bag or box to collect papers and other items that you want to keep but will sort through later. Stash knickknacks, personal photographs, and collections under your bed or in dressers. Don't put them in cupboards or drawers where potential buyers will look.

- **Set aside any extra chairs, ottomans, or other furniture that you don't use but take up prime space.** You could move them to rooms that have less furniture or use them to set up a small seating area in the basement, even if you don't usually use that area. If you simply don't have the room to display them, store them in the garage, a storage area, or in a friend's basement.

- **Clean out closet space.** Take a cardboard box to each closet and pack up shoes and clothes that will not be needed before you move. Don't leave any shoes out when showing the house.

- **Hide any signs of trouble.** Put away the bathroom plunger, mouse traps, ant bait, and so on.

- **Hide any signs of your pet.** Find a place to hide your pet's kennel, food, toys, leashes, and bowls.

- **After paring down clutter, focus on cleaning.** In the bathrooms wash the floor, clear and clean the vanity, and scrub the sink, toilet, and tub. Remove the fuzzy toilet seat cover and bath mat. If you have time later, tidy under the vanity sink.

- **Clean the kitchen.** Begin by putting small appliances under the counter if you have room. If there isn't room, pack away anything you don't need and store the labeled box in the basement or garage. Clean the counters, sink, and floor. Clear everything off the refrigerator door (magnets, pictures, etc.), and remove everything from the tops of the cabinets and the top of the refrigerator.

- **Vacuum high traffic areas.**

- **Spot clean stains on carpets and walls.**

- **Clean the front windows.** Even just a quick wipe with some cleaner and a paper towel will be an improvement.

- **Remove throw rugs and mats scattered throughout the house.** Area rugs in the living room or dining room can stay, but if you have hardwood flooring, consider removing the rugs to show it off better.

- **Place a vase of flowers on the kitchen table.** Use flowers that are white, cream, or colour-matched to your décor, and include lots of greenery. Ask a friend to babysit any tired-looking houseplants.

Once your home is listed, keep working. It will be more difficult now to properly stage your house because you need to keep it in shape to show it while you are working. Keep packing, making repairs, cleaning, and styling until your home is sold. This isn't an ideal way to prepare for a move, but it is far better than not putting any effort into staging at all.

chapter nine

Photographing, Maintaining, and Showing Your Staged House

YOU'RE FINALLY FINISHED each of the four staging steps—de-cluttering/depersonalizing, repairing/upgrading, cleaning, and styling—both inside and out. You're now ready to consult with a real estate professional to finalize your asking price, photograph your house for the online listing, and hammer that "For Sale" sign into the lawn.

After the initial euphoria of seeing your house looking renewed and show-ready, and after the bustle of photographing and posting your shots online, the new reality soon sets in: You have to actually live in your staged house and keep it looking good for last-minute showings.

That's right, once your house is staged, you have to keep it up, inside and out, for every single showing. You never know which person driving by, checking online, or attending a showing may be your potential buyer. It's important to keep your house looking freshly staged for each and every viewer in order to reap the full benefits of your hard work.

The good news is that by simply getting into a few new routines, keeping your house ship shape won't be too difficult.

This chapter guides you through the process of photographing your house for marketing it online. It also offers tips and checklists for living in and maintaining your staged house with minimal fuss. Finally, it details the last-minute preparations required for outstanding open houses and showings.

Photographing Your Staged House

Now that your house is staged, it's time to show it off.

The first place to show your house is on the Internet. By posting photos—whether on an MLS listing, your agent's website, or another real estate site—you're virtually hosting an open house 24 hours a day, seven days a week. Make sure every picture counts.

Almost everyone looking for a house in your area and price range will see your photos online before viewing the house in person and often even before talking to an agent about it. They will choose to view your house (or choose to not view it) based on what they see in the pictures. It's critical that these pictures show the house and your staging efforts at their best. Make sure high-quality photographs showcase your high-quality house.

When real estate agents are involved in the sale, they usually expect to take the pictures and post them online. However, as the homeowner, you know how important these pictures are for luring potential buyers in. After all the work you've put into staging your house, you may want to consider these pictures as a final staging effort and take them yourself, later giving them to the agent to post. If you choose not to take the pictures yourself, offer to assist the agent or to review the photos before they are posted.

Another option is to hire a real estate photographer to take the pictures for you. A professional home stager may be able to offer this service or recommend a photographer in your area.

If you take the pictures, avoid the temptation to just "point and shoot." Great real estate photos don't just happen; they require some planning, time, and effort.

- **Decide what to shoot.** Before taking pictures, first consider what shots you want to include. The host site may limit the number of photographs you can post. (However, it's not hard to get around these limitations. You could upload all the pictures you want to Flickr, Dropbox, or other hosting site and post a link to the album). At a minimum, a standard listing includes pictures of the front exterior, main living area, kitchen, eating area, formal dining room, formal living room, and master bedroom and bathroom. If the site allows more photos, include shots of the extra bedrooms and bathrooms, back yard and deck, and the basement (if it's finished). Try to include all key features. For example, does the dining room have crown molding? Make sure it's in a shot. Does the office have lovely built-in cabinets? Take a close-up of these. Does the house look onto a great view? Then be sure to include a picture of the view as well.

- **Have the right equipment.** A good digital camera with a flash is a must. If you don't have one, try to borrow one. Don't settle on using your phone or low-end camera; you won't get the quality you need. If possible, also have a tripod and a wide-angle lens. A tripod keeps the camera steady, eliminating any blur that might occur when you're holding the camera. A wide-angle lens allows you to take a picture of an entire room, rather than just a small portion of it.

- **Stage the shots.** Make sure the room or area looks just right before taking its picture. Even though the room has already been staged, you may need to make a few tweaks for the pictures. Because the posted pictures will be quite small, they can make the space look smaller and more cramped than it really is. Therefore, keep the shot clean, simple, and sparse. You may need to remove a piece of furniture or an accessory so the room doesn't look crowded. Remember to take out table extensions and extra dining room and kitchen chairs, if you haven't done so already. Make sure there are no people or pets in the picture, as they're very distracting. Also make sure to stand where your reflection will not appear in a mirror (a common oversight). It's also a good idea to remove screens on the windows before photographing the room. In the camera's eye, screens can make the windows look dark and dirty. Of course, tidy the room, pull up blinds, and fully open window treatments; in the bathrooms, close the toilet seat (another common oversight!). Before photographing the exterior of the house, move the garbage cans out of the way, clear the walkway, make sure the window coverings inside are straight, and remove vehicles from the driveway.

- **Let there be light.** Good lighting is critical for a good picture, and natural light is ideal. Open all the window coverings to allow in natural light for interior shots. However, if there's too much light from a window, the camera adjusts to this bright spot by darkening the rest of the room. Therefore, it's best to photograph interior shots on an overcast day, with all the window coverings opened. If the photos are still too dark, turn on the interior lights or try setting up an extra lamp or two directly behind you while you shoot the picture. Be careful, however, that the interior lights don't make the room appear yellow. Experiment with various lighting options until you get one that works. Try taking the pictures at different times of the day to find the best results. Exterior shots often work well on a sunny day. Shoot the picture with the sun at your back to avoid dark spots. If your house faces north, however, shooting on cloudy or overcast days helps to minimize shadows and reflective light.

- **Take the picture, again and again.** Aim for variety when photographing your rooms. Photograph the focal point or best feature of each room. If a window is a focal point, photograph it from an angle, not straight on. Take many more pictures than you think you'll need and choose the best for the website. Take pictures with a flash and without, and always use the highest resolution setting. Experiment with the optical zoom function to focus on smaller details. Move a few steps in each direction to capture a number of shots at various perspectives. Also take some shots capturing as much of the room as possible in one view. Use a wide-angle lens, or try positioning the viewfinder so that the corner of the room is in the centre of the image.

- **Edit the photos.** Once you're finished taking the pictures, choose the best ones that showcase your home's selling points, and start editing. Most pictures benefit from some editing, whether it's resizing, cropping, straightening the image, or adjusting the exposure. Many computers come with built-in photo editing software. If you don't have image editing software, download one of the many free image-editing tools available on the Internet. Some popular options include Picassa, GIMP, Picnik, and Adobe Photoshop Express.

Maintaining Your Staged House

In ideal situations, homeowners plan vacations while their house is on the market so they can leave the house and it will stay perfectly staged. Other homeowners stay with family or friends so that their house stays pristine. Most people, however, don't have these options and need to live in and maintain their staged house.

Living in a staged house can have its challenges. Much of your furniture has been removed or rearranged. Many familiar or comforting objects have been packed. And your office is so clean and organized it doesn't feel like your own.

By far the greatest challenge, however, is keeping the house this way. The second law of thermodynamics says that everything tends toward disorder, and nowhere is this more apparent than in an organized and clean house. Unless you work at upkeep, your house will eventually revert to a more disorderly and messy state.

In case you're feeling overwhelmed, don't worry. The house doesn't need to be perfect at all times. It just needs to be maintained enough so that you can quickly prepare for short-notice showings. By having already de-cluttered and deep cleaned the house, upkeep will be much simpler because you will only have to focus on surface dirt, knowing that all the nooks and crannies have recently been cleaned. And because you have already cleared out the clutter and organized your cabinets and shelves, you should always have a place to put away stray items.

You may have to add new routines to maintain your staging efforts. These new routines may become habits that you get used to doing without much thought or effort; you might even become so used to these new, good habits that you continue them in your new house.

Clutter Vigilance

Maintaining a staged house requires you to be vigilant against "clutter creep." Day-to-day clutter has a way of growing and taking over your new-found storage space. The following simple tips will help you keep your house tidy and organized:

- **Spend a little time every day putting away stray items**. Adopt a "put it away right away plan." Whether it's toys in the living room or yesterday's newspaper on the dining room table, put everything away where it belongs. Choose a time of day that works best for you—such as first thing in the morning or last thing at night—and then tidy the house at this time each day. You may want to bring a laundry basket with you as you go room by room, placing the items in the basket and then putting them away. Don't just throw things out of sight into the nearest closet. Put them away where they belong. Strive to allocate a specific place for everything. You are more likely to put it away after use if you know exactly where it belongs. (When you were de-cluttering, you found a home for every object, so this shouldn't be difficult.) If there is no good place for the item, consider whether it needs to be recycled, packed (and stored), or given away.

- **Don't bring new stuff into the house.** Unless absolutely necessary, resist the urge to buy new toys, kitchen gadgets, books, bulk goods, and so on. Remember all the work you did sorting and packing your old stuff. Don't fill all your hard-earned storage space with new stuff.

- **Use an attractive box with a lid or a basket to store miscellaneous small items.** Rather than leaving it out, contain daily clutter (keys, spare change, mail, etc.) in small decorative boxes or baskets that can later be placed out of sight, such as on a shelf in a closet. A few matching, lidded boxes can instantly hold all the day-to-day clutter from the top of your desk. Stack the boxes on the floor beside the desk. Instantly, the room appears neater and more organized. Contain your bedside materials (glasses, book, etc.) in a small box that you can store under your bed.

- **Put away cosmetics and toiletries after each use**. Keep bathrooms tidy by always putting away your cosmetics and toiletries in baskets or bins and storing them in a closed cabinet or closet. Also, every morning put away your hair dryer, brush, and even toothbrush.

- **Store your shampoos and soaps in a plastic tote that you keep in the shower.** When your agent calls with a last-minute showing, you can simply move the tote out of sight and your shower and tub will look great.

- **Keep papers under control.** This includes mail, flyers, and school paperwork. Develop a system where you manage every piece of paper as soon as it comes into the house. Start by creating one place in the house (your inbox) for all incoming paperwork. Don't just toss papers on the table, dresser, or wherever you happen to be, hoping to get to them later. As soon paperwork makes it to the inbox, immediately recycle all junk mail. After a few days or a week, sort through your inbox and process the papers. Pay the bills immediately, file papers that you need to keep (in the filing system you've already set up), and transfer information from the paper (such as activities or important dates) onto your calendar. Once you've processed each piece of paper, immediately file or recycle the paper.

- **Keep kitchen counters free of extra appliances.** Unless you plan to leave the item out to stage the counter, get into the habit of putting appliances and utensils away in cabinets or drawers.

If your home stays on the market for longer than you had hoped, spend 30 minutes each month walking through your home and gathering items that you can pack away or donate to a charity.

Daily and Weekly Cleaning Routines

Keeping that freshly staged look involves daily and weekly cleaning. Doing a little bit often will not only keep your house looking great, it will also save you time and effort before showings.

Keep a tote or box of basic cleaning supplies (all-purpose cleaner, glass cleaner, disinfectant wipes, paper towel, and microfiber cloths or rags) in the kitchen and bathrooms so that they're handy whenever you get the chance to use them. (Make sure to store them out of sight.)

Aim to spend about a half an hour a day cleaning the house. While you're cleaning, open some windows and turn on the bathroom fans for a few minutes to air out the house and keep it smelling fresh. See the checklist at the end of this chapter for a summary of daily cleaning chores.

Once every week, focus on deeper cleaning. Don't worry; you won't need to work as hard as you did when you initially staged your house. See the checklist at the end of this chapter for a summary of weekly cleaning chores. Delegate tasks to each member of the household, or if it's within your budget, hire a weekly cleaning service.

Quick Tips for Maintaining a Staged House

Keeping a house looking freshly staged will help you to always be prepared for last-minute showings. As well doing the daily cleaning chores included in the checklist, you can also make some simple changes to your routine to help keep the picture-perfect look maintained.

- If you have more than one bathroom in your house, and if it's practical, designate one for use and leave the others clean and ready for showings.
- Walk the dog frequently. Taking your dog for daily walks will help preserve your lawn and keep your yard (ahem) cleaner.

- If you and your family usually use the front door as your main entrance but also have a back entrance, use the back entrance until the house is sold to keep the front clean. Also store coats, footwear, and backpacks at the back door to keep the front entrance neat.

- In order to better manage toys, designate one play area in the home. Encourage lots of outdoor playtime, if possible. For the time being, ask for play dates to be held at friends' houses rather than your own.

- Prepare simple meals that won't require a lot of work and clean up. Many people choose to make life simpler while their house is on the market by forgoing entertaining and elaborate meals. Pull out your crock-pot. Consider preparing meals in large batches and freezing some for use later. If it's within your budget, spend more on prepared meals and eating out.

- Be careful of what you cook while your house is on the market. Strong smell can be big deterrents, and cooking odors tend to linger. Until your house is sold, avoid cooking with strong smelling foods or seasonings, including cabbage, garlic, curry, and fish.

- Keep replacing cut flowers so they are fresh for showings. Remember, they needn't be large, costly arrangements. One type of flower (in one colour) with lots of greenery from your local grocery store is perfectly acceptable. Or display single blooms in a row of three small vases.

- Hang everyday towels over top of new, neatly folded towels. When it's time for a showing, remove your used towels to reveal the fresh ones underneath. Another option is to fold your display towels so that they are ready for showings and then neatly store them in the linen closet until they are needed.

- If something breaks, repair it right away or contact someone who can repair it for you.

- Replace burned-out light bulbs immediately.

- If you have a damp basement, run a dehumidifier when you are not showing your house. Turn it off and tuck it out of sight for showings.

- If someone in the house smokes, have a strict policy that all smoking must be done outside. Remember to clean up all evidence that a smoker lives there (e.g., put away ashtrays and clean up any butts left outside).

Showing Your House

After all the effort you put into staging your house and keeping it staged, you'll welcome the chance to finally be able to show it to potential buyers. Open houses, scheduled showings, and last-minute drop-ins are all opportunities to sell your house. Make the most of each opportunity.

The key to being prepared for showings is to have a plan ready beforehand. Assign tasks for each family member ahead of time so that everyone knows what to do when you get the call.

Have a plan for what you'll do with your pets when you're showing your house. All pets (except fish) should be out of the house during a showing or open house. Either arrange to take your pet to a friend or relative's house during the showing, or plan to take it with you in the car. Also hide obvious evidence of your pets by removing food and water dishes, kennels, leashes, litter boxes, etc. If you don't have a better place for these items, stow them in the trunk of your car as you leave the house.

When you're notified that someone wants to view your home, have everyone spring into action. Concentrate on the areas that will be seen first, which are usually the front entry, living room, kitchen, and dining room. Move to the bathrooms next, followed by the bedrooms. Attend to the remaining areas if you have time.

The following is a list of last-minute tasks to do immediately before showing your house:

- **Maximize the light.** Plenty of light is essential for a good showing. As you prepare each room, turn on each and every light, even for daytime showings. If you're going to be at work before the showing, turn the lights on before you leave the house. Also pull drapes back from the window and stack the blinds to the top of the windows to let in plenty of light. For evening showings, it's still best to pull back all the drapes to showcase the window; you can pull the blinds down for a cozy look, but keep the slats opened. Also turn on the outside lights for late afternoon and evening showings. Light battery-operated candles if you have them. In the fall and winter, turn on the gas fireplace. If you have a wood-burning fireplace, leave a tidy stack of cut wood inside it.

- **Freshen the air naturally.** Open some windows for a few minutes, even in winter, to let fresh air in. It's best to do this at least an hour before the showing so that you'll have time to regulate the temperature. If you're struggling to rid your home of an unpleasant smell, try lighting beeswax candles, which have a natural, subtle honey scent. (Make sure to extinguish them before leaving.) You can also freshen the air by boiling a tablespoon of vinegar in a cup of water. Or, try adding 2 tablespoons of cinnamon and some orange peels to a cup of water and boil for 10 to 15 minutes. If there's a bag of smelly hockey gear or offensive running shoes in a closet, move them to the garage or the trunk of your car.

- **Put away daily clutter.** Gather all the small, personal items that accumulate or are left out every day (e.g., keys, change, mail, medications, etc.). Place these in a drawer, or if you've been containing them in a box, move the box to an out-of-way location. Also hide your tissue boxes and calendars (if you've recorded your appointments on them).

- **Tidy the entrance way first.** Put jackets and shoes in the closet. Spot clean the floor as needed.

- **Stand at the doorway and look into your home.** Quickly put away anything that is out of place. Make sure high traffic areas are clear. Move any chairs or tables, if necessary, to ensure buyers will be able to walk easily through the room.

- **Tidy the living room and family room.** Fluff pillows and straighten any throws. Hide the remote, newspapers, magazines, and toys. If you're very short on time and have many items out of place, take a large bag and collect anything that you can't quickly return to its rightful place. Hide this bag under your bed (if it has a bed skirt), in a bin in your basement or garage, or take it with you in your car when you leave for the showing. Remember to return all items to their right places after the showing.

- **Prepare the kitchen.** Clear and clean countertops, the sink, and the tabletop. Close all cabinet doors, and empty the garbage. Quickly check that the surfaces of the appliances are clean, especially the stovetop and the refrigerator door. Make sure that the floor is clean.

- **Tidy the dining room.** Make sure the table is clear and clean, and push the chairs completely under the table. Remove extra leaves and chairs, if you haven't done so already.

- **Bathrooms are next.** Use disinfecting wipes to clean bathroom counters, sinks, and toilet. Dry the bathtub and shower. Move the shower tote filled with your soaps and shampoos out of sight. Make sure there are no toiletries left out on the counter, and empty the garbage. Remove your day-to-day towels and display your neatly folded fresh towels. Put the toilet seat down. (Bathrooms look much classier when the toilet seat is down!). Remove the bath mat to make the room more spacious. Hide the toilet brush, bathroom scale, and toilet plunger; for buyers, these signal work, weight, and worry.

- **Check the bedrooms**. Make sure the beds are made. Fluff the pillows. Put away stray toys and dirty clothes. Close closet doors. Open all window coverings and turn on the lights.

- **Next, attend to the laundry area.** Don't leave laundry in the washer or dryer because potential buyers may look inside. Fold a towel neatly over baskets of clean, dirty, or wet laundry in order to keep it out of easy view. Wipe the top of the washer and dryer.

- **Vacuum high traffic areas.**

- **Make sure the house is a comfortable temperature.**

- **Arrange vignettes.** If you had planned on creating a vignette, do it now. However, don't make the exact same vignettes used in your photos.

- **Display fresh flowers**. If you have the time, set out fresh flowers in the kitchen/dining area, living room, and all bathrooms. These will also make the house fragrant.

- **Leave a copy of your home inspection report or printed information about your house**. If you have these, it's a nice touch to leave them on a table for potential buyers to review.

- **Set out a treat**. If you have time, set a tray of muffins or cookies on your counter with a few water bottles or a pot of coffee. Leave a note welcoming potential buyers to help themselves.

- **Attend to curb appeal**. Double check that everything in the front yard is in order (e.g., make sure there are no toys, bikes, yard tools, or other items lying in the yard). Sweep or shovel the walkway, if necessary, for a welcoming entrance. Pick up after your dog. Move the garbage can and recycling bins away from the front of the house. Remove vehicles from your garage and driveway and park them down the street instead of in front of your home. Close the garage door.

Congratulations! You have now set the stage for quick and profitable sale.

Daily Cleaning CHECKLIST

Kitchen

❑ Wash and put away dishes after every meal.

❑ Wipe counters.

❑ Empty garbage.

❑ Clean and shine the kitchen sink and faucet.

❑ Wipe down the stovetop after each use.

❑ Wipe backsplash over the stove after cooking.

❑ Sweep or vacuum the floor.

❑ Spot clean sticky or dirty areas on the floor.

❑ Wipe up all spills while they're fresh to prevent staining.

❑ Wipe up grease and splatters in your oven and microwave after each use.

❑ Fold and hang dishtowels.

❑ Clear the kitchen table and wipe it down.

Bathrooms

❑ Empty trash.

❑ Wipe down the sink and mirror.

❑ Wipe down the tub and shower—a thorough cleaning isn't necessary; you only need to wipe up water drops to make it look presentable.

❑ Spread out the shower curtain and liner to prevent mildew.

❑ Wipe down the shower door with a squeegee or towel to remove water drops.

❑ Clean the toilet seat and rim.

Bedrooms

❑ Put dirty clothes in the hamper.

❑ Fold or hang up clean clothes.

- ❑ Put away ties, jewelry, shoes, etc.
- ❑ Make the bed and fluff the pillows.
- ❑ Straighten the bedside table; put away extra items that have made their way there.
- ❑ In children's rooms, put away toys, books, and other stray items left on the floor.

Living Area
- ❑ Straighten the pillows on the sofa.
- ❑ Fold and reposition throws.
- ❑ Do a quick vacuum if needed.
- ❑ Remove fingerprints or smudges from cabinets and glass surfaces.
- ❑ Straighten items on coffee table and end tables.
- ❑ Return stray items to their proper places.

Laundry
- ❑ Do the laundry daily if there are several people in the household. Have all members of the household help, especially with folding and putting the laundry away every day.

Front and Back Yards
- ❑ Water flowers daily or as needed.
- ❑ Put away toys, bikes, and other items.
- ❑ Clean up after your dog.
- ❑ Shovel or sweep walkways and driveway, as needed.

Weekly Cleaning CHECKLIST

Kitchen

- ❑ Dust light fixtures.

- ❑ Wipe down the garbage can and clean the area around it.

- ❑ Clean the exteriors of all appliances, making sure to remove fingerprints.

- ❑ Discard expired foods and wipe down the interior of the fridge.

- ❑ Vacuum and mop the floor.

- ❑ Spot clean cabinets, walls, and windows, as needed.

Bathrooms

- ❑ Launder towels.

- ❑ Clean and disinfect toilets, sinks, mirrors, tubs, and showers.

- ❑ Dust light fixtures.

- ❑ Spot clean cabinets and walls.

- ❑ Empty garbage and wipe down garbage can.

- ❑ Vacuum and mop floors.

- ❑ Vacuum exhaust vents.

Bedrooms

- ❑ Change and launder pillowcases.

- ❑ Dust surfaces, including bedside tables, dressers, and light fixtures.

- ❑ Vacuum floors.

Living Areas and Throughout the House

- ❑ Dust all surfaces, including electronics, shelves, and items on the shelves.

- ❑ Polish wood surfaces, removing fingerprints.

- ❑ Dust light fixtures.

- ☐ Spot clean windows, walls, and glass doors, as needed.
- ☐ Remove cobwebs from corners and the ceiling.
- ☐ Dust baseboards.
- ☐ Vacuum and mop floors.

Front Yard

- ☐ Mow the grass (at least weekly; twice a week if necessary).
- ☐ Weed flowerbeds.
- ☐ Sweep or shovel walkways and driveway.
- ☐ Remove ice around downspouts and on walkways, if needed.
- ☐ Remove dirt and cobwebs from front entry area, mailbox, and light fixtures.

De-Cluttering Decision Tree

Consider the following questions when you have difficulty deciding what to keep in the house and what to pack (and store), give away, sell, or trash.

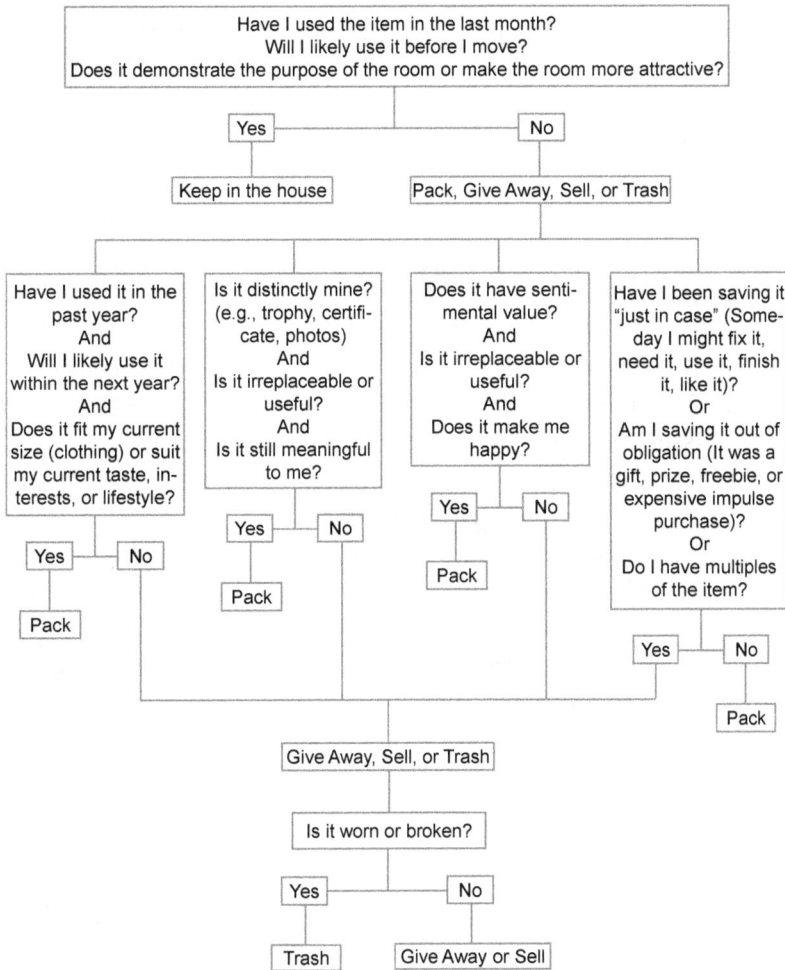

Have I used the item in the last month?
Will I likely use it before I move?
Does it demonstrate the purpose of the room or make the room more attractive?

Yes — No

Keep in the house

Pack, Give Away, Sell, or Trash

Have I used it in the past year?
And
Will I likely use it within the next year?
And
Does it fit my current size (clothing) or suit my current taste, interests, or lifestyle?

Yes — No

Pack

Is it distinctly mine? (e.g., trophy, certificate, photos)
And
Is it irreplaceable or useful?
And
Is it still meaningful to me?

Yes — No

Pack

Does it have sentimental value?
And
Is it irreplaceable or useful?
And
Does it make me happy?

Yes — No

Pack

Have I been saving it "just in case" (Someday I might fix it, need it, use it, finish it, like it)?
Or
Am I saving it out of obligation (It was a gift, prize, freebie, or expensive impulse purchase)?
Or
Do I have multiples of the item?

Yes — No

Pack

Give Away, Sell, or Trash

Is it worn or broken?

Yes — No

Trash

Give Away or Sell

A Final Word

THINK OF THE LAST TIME you went to a live performance. When the lights came on and you had your first view of the empty stage waiting for the performers, were you immediately drawn into the event, even before a word was said? If you were, it's because the stage was set to create the right mood and atmosphere. It was the perfect backdrop for the show to come alive.

That's the same type of magical effect that home staging has. It sets just the right scene for people dreaming of their future home: they will be able to imagine moving in and having everything they and their family want and need to live comfortably.

Staging creates a spacious, bright, clean, orderly, and welcoming environment. It highlights the best features of your house and eliminates or minimizes issues that could jeopardize a sale. Through staging, you take what may have been a perfectly good home for you and make it into a dream home for a large and diverse audience.

We wish you the best of luck with the sale of your home. We hope that, like many other homeowners who stage their houses, you feel proud of your staged home and enjoy the positive feedback once you're done. Best of all, you can rest assured that you have dramatically increased your odds of a quick and profitable sale!

Acknowledgements

THIS BOOK IS THE RESULT OF A LIFE-LONG FRIENDSHIP, two moms with an idea, and the melding of the talents of a home stager and an editor. We are grateful for each other's invaluable contributions to the creation of this book.

We owe a special thanks to Danny Classen for the countless hours he donated creating the superb photography used throughout the book. Thank you also to Hans Holtkamp for his exceptional work photographing the front cover.

We also are very grateful for the words of wisdom graciously provided by James Rayner (cavasecreta.ca); Christine Korchinski (christinesdrapery.ca); Brandy O'Brien and Joline Throssell; Pauline Beres; Barb Wouters (woutersrealty.com); Ron Baliski (teambaliski.com); Kelly Oleksyn (mosaicdevelopments.ca); Carla Sharback (blossomsliving.ca); Brenda W. Couros (K. Ash & Co. Development); and Melanie Orvold.

Our special thanks go to Carla Sharback and her staff at Blossoms Living, who welcomed us into their store to photograph the cover. Not only did Carla allow us to use any of her gorgeous selection of furniture and accessories, she also assisted with setting up the shot.

Joanne would like to thank everyone who greatly improved this book by reading early drafts and offering their insightful suggestions: Suzanne Classen, Maureen Dinnen, Norma McKercher, Lee Mazurick, Yvette Nolan, and Ryan Sanche.

Shannon would like to acknowledge her supportive family, special friends, and the wonderful women with whom she stages properties. In particular, sincere appreciation goes to Norma McKercher for her many talents and wise mentorship over the years.

www.ingramcontent.com/pod-product-compliance
Lightning Source LLC
Chambersburg PA
CBHW060029210326
41520CB00009B/1060